The Darkness

Permission To Rock

Dick Porter

Plexus, London

Published by Plexus Publishing Limited
London SW4 9BX
Tel: 020 7622 2440
Fax: 020 7622 2441
www.plexusbooks.com
First printing 2004

British Libary Cataloguing in Publication Data

Porter, Dick
The Darkness : permission to rock
1.Darkness (Group) 2.Rock musicians - Great
Britain - Biography
I.Title
782.4'2166'0922

ISBN 0 85965 352 8

Cover and Book Design by Brian Flynn
Cover photograph by Simon Songhurst/Camera Press
Printed in Great Britain by Scotprint, Haddington

Half title page: Justin by Sarahphotogirl;
Frontispiece: Ed, Frankie, Dan and Justin crack
open a bottle to toast the success of 'Permission
To Land' by Steve Double/Retna;
Contents page: Justin by Sarahphotogirl

Contents

The

1

East Anglian Rhapsody

The Darkness are four men, men's men. Your basic macho, masculine, testosterone driven, muscular, tall, handsome, chiselled, square jawed, large chinned men. Three of whom are from Lowestoft. One is Scottish. **Justin Hawkins**

In the final weeks of 2002, the buzz that had been growing around The Darkness reached ear-splitting proportions. For a band who had, at one time or another, been dismissed as a joke, ignored by the music press, and laboured on without the benefit of a record deal, this success was well overdue. Since their inception, nearly three years earlier, The Darkness had refused to perceive themselves as anything other than stadium-rock-gods-in-waiting.

As charismatic front man Justin Hawkins explained, 'For many moons, we have been bracing ourselves for a shift in the public's perception of The Darkness from underdogs to world-beaters. Our debut album will undoubtedly be a catalyst for this transition. About time, too!'

Justin was as prescient as he is handsome – within weeks, *Permission To Land* had gone to the top of the UK chart and the band had sold out venues across Britain, Ireland and the USA. Sections of the music press were proclaiming 2003 the 'Year of the Darkness', and it was scarcely possible to turn on the radio without hearing Justin's distinctive ultrasonic warble. Augmenting him on vocals and guitar, his younger brother Dan (guitar), Frankie Poullain (bass) and Ed Graham (drums) saw out the year poised to make good on their vow of 'global domination'.

Thumbs Up! Justin salutes Glastonbury, June 2003.

Freddie Mercury resplendent in a catsuit. Queen are of course a key influence on the Darkness.

Known as the first town in mainland Britain to welcome the rays of the dawn sun, it's ironic that the East Anglian tourist resort of Lowestoft also gave rise to The Darkness. Three quarters of the band (Justin, Dan and Ed) grew up in the former medieval fishing village and attended the nearby Kirkley High School (motto: *I ought, therefore I can. I can, therefore I will*).

Like most brothers, Dan and Justin had regular bust ups, but, as Justin explained, they're hardly the Gallaghers: 'We're not really like traditional band brothers, we have had our moments, but it's kind of, everyone's a bit conflict shy and we try and resolve things in as much of a reasonable way as possible without fisticuffs or glassing because we're both very hard. It's a tough call actually 'cos Dan's very determined, but I'm fit, he's got a big beer gut and obviously that gives him the leverage but I'm fast and I'm quite accurate.'

At school, Dan found himself in the same class as Ed Graham. The future drummer was less ostentatious or precocious than Justin, nor was he as charming and diligent as Dan. Whereas the infant Justin was labelled 'a screamer' by his mother and an 'immature attention seeker' by teachers, Ed was quixotic and introspective – preferring to focus on painting his award-winning lead figures. As their former history teacher, Mr. Spencer, recalls, 'With Justin, I'll always remember that he was a lively, articulate, sort of zany character. He used to have a whacko sense of humour even then. Dan was much quieter, probably steadier. Ed, I didn't know as well, his mind was into the music, drums all the time . . .'

Ed's interest in drumming served to strengthen his bond with Justin and Dan, both of whom were also developing a keen interest in music. 'I knew from an early age exactly what I wanted to do,' recalls Dan. 'I wanted to be a musician and that was it. It made life a lot easier knowing what I was aiming for.'

Encouraged by their parents, whose favourites included Bob Dylan, Led Zeppelin, Queen and Blondie, the Hawkins brothers set about acquiring the palette of influences and skills that would colour their musical development. 'All stuff like Fleetwood Mac and Queen [was] through my Dad. When I developed my own taste it was all Aerosmith and Van Halen,' acknowledges Justin. Like his two friends, Ed came from a musically orientated household. His older brother, Andy, fronted a local band, the Gypzy Tartz, who later became Crush, releasing an album titled *Invisible* in 1996.

Back at school, Justin demonstrated some of the flamboyant behaviour that was to become his trademark as a performer, and to get him labelled 'a total pain in the arse' by his brother. Electing to arrive for the day's lessons with his underpants worn, Superman style, outside his trousers, he more than earned the nickname 'Y-Fronts Man'.

We were quite naturally twats for a long time but now we are considered cool for some reason. Dan Hawkins

As Justin later explained to the *Guardian*, he wasn't overly concerned with street credibility. 'We were fucking losers,' he admitted. 'The world has changed around us. We are still the biggest twats you are likely to encounter, but for some reason that is all the rage now.'

A definite distance from the trendiness of his peers set Justin apart from the crowd. More interested in the poodle-metal of bands like Van Halen and Thunder than the latest house and garage releases, he grew his hair and adopted the greatcoat and scarf look guaranteed to make him a social leper.

'I'm Justin Hawkins and I'm going to be a rock 'n' roll star,' he'd introduce himself. Whilst ultimately accurate, it was hardly likely to win many friends. Reflecting upon the perils of his individualism, Justin revealed, 'You had to walk through the town centre knowing that round any corner you might get jumped on because of the way you dressed and the music you listened to.'

Denied the opportunity of 'sitting under the pier with the cool kids,' it was a small mercy when Harry and Sandy Hawkins provided their boys with a productive outlet for their enthusiasm. 'They had an outside toilet block,' recalled Ed, 'and their dad is a builder and he converted the outside toilet into a rehearsal room.'

'We were quite lucky,' Dan observed. 'When we go back home and talk to the kids in bands there at the moment, they say they have nowhere to play. If we really do hit the big time, one thing we would like to do is to fund some kind of studio where they can go and practice.'

The first fruit of Mr. and Mrs. Hawkins' £2,000-investment in their offspring was a late-1980s covers band called Vital Signs. Specialising in the hits of Queen and Marillion, the ensemble featured Dan on lead vocals with Justin on guitar. The group performed at family gatherings and social occasions, providing Justin with sufficient experience to hook up with local rockers Biff! – then trying to make a name for themselves by touring local pubs in a van called 'Betsy'.

As former Biff! member Steve Hobbs explains, 'In those days, the pinnacle of all our ambitions was to receive groupie love, post-gig, behind a stack of speaker cabinets while heading home along the A12. I had even managed to come to terms with the fact that Justin was a far better guitar player than

AC/DC guitarist Angus Young goes walkabout, on lead singer Brian Johnson's shoulders, a move inherited by Justin.

346 CH

me, despite his having only been playing for a year. And, oddly, he was often so shy offstage that we didn't even know he could sing, but there was this weird piercing warble he would occasionally emit when drinking beer. Or pissing around at sound-checks. The plan was a simple one, we would move to London, live on the dole and play anywhere we could until people started to take notice. Such was my commitment; I had even deferred my university place for a whole year. Only, unknown to any of us, our singer had been quietly crooning at my brother's girlfriend. When he finally discovered what was going on, in the middle of our show-stopping thrash-metal rendition of "Lucy In The Sky With Diamonds", he leapt over his drum kit and punched the erstwhile vocalist off the stage. They never spoke again – so, disillusioned, I filled Betsy with camping equipment and a hippy, dippy girlfriend and spent the year off travelling Europe instead. Justin, meanwhile, went and got his first tattoo and continued with the plan alone.'

Following the demise of Biff! in 1991, Justin's 'plan' involved about three years of signing-on in Lowestoft and working on his Brian May/Angus Young techniques. Whilst Ed worked for a more mundane branch of the music industry, on the local Sanyo production line, Dan decided to relocate to form a new band.

It's all very well Eminem going on about Detroit. You have to be a bit braver to go around singing the praises of Lowestoft. **Justin Hawkins**

'[Dan] moved to London when he was seventeen,' Sandy Hawkins explains. 'He finally got this band together, he joined it actually, then proceeded to sack everyone and he was left on his own. Daniel has always been the serious hard working one, an actual perfectionist if you like. Justin has just floated around and couldn't care less about anything much, including school.'

Justin's aversion to academic work was finally overcome by the sheer boredom of being stuck at home. In 1995 he enrolled in a two-year music technology course at Highfields Technical College, Huddersfield. Just as at Kirkley High, his sartorial extravagance soon got him noticed.

'He dressed a bit like Austin Powers, or Mike Flowers, the spoof sixties singer,' lecturer Charlie Griffiths recalls. 'He'd wear brown jackets with big lapels and he had a Jarvis Cocker hairdo. It wasn't until he took part in an end-of-year concert that his metal leanings came to the fore. Justin donned a long black wig to sing in his now-trademark falsetto for the fun gig. He was just like Ian Gillan from Deep Purple! It was outrageous!'

Since dismissing his first London-based band, Dan had begun picking up some session work for performers like Natale Imbruglia. As he observes, 'I was playing with a load of amazing musicians who'd done some really big stuff, been in massive bands in the eighties, but they hadn't made enough money to have a living. They're still really into it, but it's like a job and they never wanted it to be like that. I don't think I could go back to session stuff after this band. I'd rather not play at all than play for some funk outfit.'

Keen to head out on his own heavy-metal highway, Dan placed an ad in the music press for some (hopefully) less disappointing musicians. One hopeful respondent was Frankie Poullain, a bassist from Scotland some six years Dan's senior. The pair hit it off and began jamming together, before taking up joint residence in a Shepherd's Bush flat. Poullain presented himself as something of a man of mystery, claiming his father had been a pirate in the

Early days – the band struggle to cram all their gear into the Darkness-mobile.

West Indies and his brother was a soldier of fortune. In reality, Frankie's background was quite interesting enough: his father was an itinerant musician who abandoned his wife and child, while his stepbrother is the situationist comedian and writer Phil Kay. Although he has never publicly identified his father, Frankie has stated, 'I will talk to him only once The Darkness have sold a million records. I admit I'm driven by a need to prove something to him, but I'm also doing it for my mum, who brought me up on her own.'

Dan and Frankie's west London flat provided the ideal venue for the extended jam sessions much beloved of out-of-work musicians. Both Justin and Ed were regular visitors, and took full part in these free-form jamborees. Fresh from graduating with his National Diploma, Justin was looking for something but remained sceptical about being in a band with his younger brother. However, his distaste for the dreary prospect of returning to Lowestoft outweighed this reluctance, and in mid-1997 he relocated to the capital.

'I don't like people very much so I couldn't be arsed with it,' he later confessed. 'I joined in the end but at that time I was just the synthesiser player.' Justin's qualifications helped him to make inroads into advertising, with his most enduring achievement in the field being the Ikea 'Schlomping' ad jingle – named as the third most annoying advert of 2002 by *Marketing* magazine.

Whereas Frankie was the obvious choice to play bass, Ed's decision to remain in Suffolk led to the band enduring a procession of short-lived and unmemorable drummers. The line up was completed by an equally temporary vocalist known simply as Paul. The quintet settled on the name 'Empire', embracing a poppy interpretation of prog-rock with Dan on lead guitar and Justin on guitar and keyboards.

The band began gigging in London and were fortunate enough to be noticed by the former Verve manager, John Best. Encouraged by his assistant, Sue Whitehouse, Best put some money into Empire and the band looked as if they might be going places. Except that they weren't.

As an unnamed source later told *NME*, 'They just weren't very good. No one was interested, the look was very different – the hair was short and they didn't have the tattoos. It was way more polite. The singer had a white soul voice, a bit like George Michael.'

Changes were made –Paul was sacked and an advertisement placed in *Melody Maker* for a replacement. Abandoning the keyboards, Justin began to guide the group in a heavier direction. The rock aesthetic that became the cornerstone of The Darkness first manifested at the Backstreet Studios audition sessions. Although well-attended, the band became increasingly dissatisfied with the standard of applicant. Their playing became progressively heavier and louder, until the amps were cranked up to stadium levels with the express intention of 'blowing the heads off' of the sub-standard singers.

Empire's switch to pure rock was obviously a key point in the genesis of The Darkness. However, bereft of such hindsight, John Best was rapidly losing faith in his investment. From his perspective, it had been nearly two years since the quintet had formed and there was a distinct lack of anything actually happening.

'They just frittered away my money,' he later complained. 'I can't even remember what they sounded like, but I don't think they were up to much.' Dismayed by the lack of any kind of return from the band, and unsettled by the way that the 'very tall' Frankie Poullain was 'always hanging around the office', Best dropped Empire.

Starved of funding, the group limped on, with Sue Whitehouse taking over as manager. In addition to her professional commitment, she had embarked on a relationship with Justin – which was kept secret from the rest of the band until 2002. A further blow was struck to Empire's fading dreams when Frankie announced he was leaving to spend the dawn of the

The wildman of rock reveals his tender side for a photo shoot.

JUSTIN

Tamla

new millennium with his brother in Venezuela, where he eventually found work as a tour guide for visiting Danish students. Without a singer, bassist or permanent drummer, there was effectively no longer any group.

The fact that Justin was receiving a decent income from his advertising work was little consolation, and Dan viewed a return to session work as potentially 'a bit soul destroying'. As the twentieth century approached its much-hyped conclusion, Justin and Dan returned to Lowestoft to consider how, and if, they were to continue as a band.

Justin demonstrates his axe virtuosity.

It's Dan's turn to be moody and sensitive...

2

For Those About To Rock

I think our motto is 'Why stop there?' or 'If something's worth doing, it's worth over doing.' **Justin Hawkins**

Like much of Britain, Dan and Justin Hawkins viewed the arrival of the third millennium through the bottom of a glass. Whereas the bulk of the population awoke with little more than a sore head, the brothers Hawkins greeted the new century with a fresh impetus.

The duo had joined the rest of the family for a New Year's Eve party at their auntie's pub – the Swan in Gillingham, near Beccles on the Norfolk/Suffolk border. Being a musical lot, there was no shortage of singing and dancing. For his party piece, Justin offered a staggering performance of interpretative movement and ersatz aerobics to Queen's 'Bohemian Rhapsody'.

Bare-chested and fuelled only by the majesty of rock and the power of the local ale, he delighted family and friends with his sparkling repertoire of star-jumps and vocal contortionism. For Dan, it was something of an epiphany. 'We were all getting pissed, and Justin and I were laughing at our dad dancing,' he recalls. 'And then Justin did his turn, basically singing and doing contemporary dance to "Bohemian Rhapsody", and it was the funniest thing I've ever seen. But at the same time I was nodding my head and smiling and rocking . . . Straight after that we decided to form this band.'

The enthusiastic response to Justin's performance was not lost on Dan – the metaphorical light bulb above his head lit up as he turned to his older brother and said, 'I know – *you* be the front man!' It also marked the beginning of the band's mythology.

Justin launches himself to dramatic effect at the Isle of Wight festival, May 2003.

Duelling Les Pauls – The Hawkins brothers get down, October 2002.

In fact, the accepted myth would be that the band had emerged from some kind of festive karaoke gala. 'We are not competition winners!' insists Justin. 'I did not sing karaoke! It is officially a lie! Yes, it was Millennium eve, my family was there and I just danced for them. I used my body to punctuate the lyrical content of that song. And it was good!'

'We just told the story in an interview and then it became, "How the band was started,"' admits Dan.

Although the two-year hunt for an appropriate vocalist was at an end, the nascent band was still short of a rhythm section. Frankie was summoned back from Venezuela for another shot at the big time. Despite the Empire debacle, the enigmatic bassist responded immediately – 'There was no way in the world I was going to miss being a part of The Darkness,' he'd later claim.

Drums were to be provided by Ed Graham, who also had the advantage of being closer to hand. The drummer had spent the last six months playing with local outfit Q*Sling, but quickly discharged his commitments to hook up with his oldest mates. It was also Ed who provided the newly-formed band with its name.

Whereas Justin is ebullient and charming, Dan engaging and articulate, and Frankie windswept and interesting, Ed is brooding and introspective. Like many teenagers, he was prone to bouts of sullen moodiness. 'He went through a bad, depressed phase as a student, and we'd say, "Ed's getting The Darkness again,"' revealed Dan. 'We named ourselves after Ed's mind. It felt right. It's better than being named after a Tim Buckley LP.'

'The Darkness just seemed to fit,' concurred Justin, 'and I can't picture us being called anything else now.'

People are going to shit themselves when they hear us . . . because Frankie's Zen bass lines oscillate at a frequency that increases bowel movements, so the best thing to do is to go to the toilet before we come on – that way you won't have any accidents. **Justin Hawkins**

With Frankie having exchanged life as the Don Juan of the Venezuelan tourist industry for a Belsize Park bedsit and a pushbike, the rest of The Darkness returned to London to begin rehearsals. Sue Whitehouse returned as manager, and the band set about honing their sound and image with renewed intent.

Up until now, Justin had been a staunch advocate of the beer-and-curry-diet. But now, he undertook a rigorous programme to hone his physique into the lithe hardbody befitting a rock god. 'When we started the band we were like Meatloaf 'cos I was a big boy, a fat boy y'know,' he later confessed. 'With a combination of regular exercise and bulimia I managed to fight that. We all believe that we were born to do this and the people that liked us also thought that too. So it's very clear that more people think that when you look like you were born to do it. We tried for ages to get Frankie to shave his moustache off, he's been cultivating that thing since middle school.'

With their image gradually forming, the emphasis switched to their sound. 'We went more in a rock direction when I became the singer. We had no choice – AC/DC are the best live band ever,' asserts Justin 'I've managed to force a lot of my eighties rock ideals on to the rest of the band, which really helps when you're trying to fit three solos into one song! It's what sets us apart really. Soloing makes your balls feel bigger, doesn't it?'

Determined to stand out from the herd of sub-Radiohead miserablists and nu-metal-by-numbers bands clogging up the millennial music scene, Justin looked to stadium-rock for direction. 'It's my musical heritage . . . what I used to listen to as a child. There ain't a lot of it around! It's a return to our roots really, rather than swim with the other fishes, make your own pool.'

'Everyone's too uptight these days,' agreed Frankie. 'I hate the arrogance of bands who think their petty emotions are interesting. If you look at bands from 25 years ago, people have smiles on their faces. We're bringing a bit of that back.'

'Half the reason that all the teenagers in black-hooded tops are so miserable is that they don't have any music that allows them to feel happy,' added Dan.

With a full-blown rock manifesto now in place, The Darkness set about creating the material that would transmute their ambitions into sonic reality.

Band and crew aboard the Leeds Festival backstage buggy, August 2003.

The creative demarcation lines were swiftly drawn. 'On a song by song basis I'm more head of the pie, just call me the crust master. If someone has something that's good then it happens and we are all credited for that,' explained Justin. 'Dan writes the majority of the music but everyone has a very valuable input.'

We're prepared not to make money for years. **Frankie Poullain**

Whilst formulating their new direction, the band undertook their first live performance at a benefit gig in Camden on 26 February 2000. The show was aimed at raising money for the family of Q*Sling bassist Sam Powell, who had committed suicide at the beginning of the year. Despite the sadness of the occasion, the band seized the opportunity to strut their new stuff – 'it was a full-on rock assault,' recalls Justin.

The band laboured on throughout the spring and summer, honing their twin-guitar sound and anthemic riffs to performance level. As their set gradually came together, the Hawkins brothers manifested their own unique creative synergy. 'I think that we realised that Dan and I could be a winning combination, a driven, serious person and a total twat,' observed Justin. 'This is our one shot at being a "family" band.'

In addition to refining a six-pack stomach out of something more redolent of a keg ('I went on a huge regime of six months talking about how little I was drinking'), Justin had undertaken a program of vocal exercises aimed at enhancing both his range and stamina, an organic process that had begun in Empire. 'I did backing vocals before which had to be higher than the main bloke's anyway because I was harmonising with him and he was a quite high singer,'

Real rock, with muscles – Justin shows his wild side, October 2002.

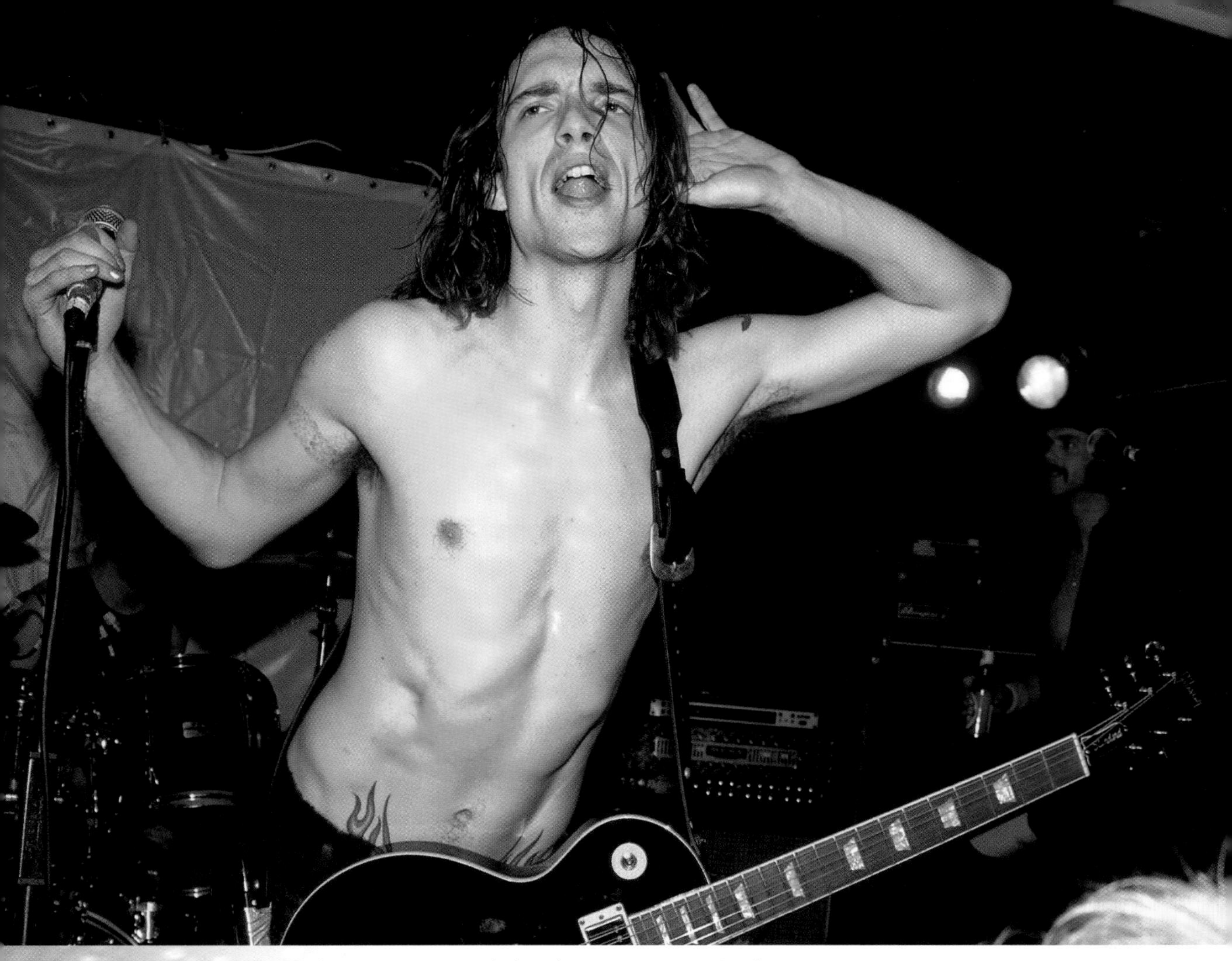

'I can't hear you…' – Justin engages in a little audience participation, October 2002.

Justin explained. 'It's the loudest part of my voice. In any rehearsal environment, you can get yourself heard by squealing.'

The Darkness's earliest material contained such now-forgotten classics as 'Sushi', 'Hell's Gazelle' and 'Nothing's Gonna Stop Us Now' – a song that celebrated the band's beery genesis. Although much of the band's appeal lies in a certain overblown absurdity, a number in praise of a satanic antelope was considered simply *too* silly, and dropped from the set.

'We were convinced that a gazelle was a bit like a jaguar,' confessed Dan. 'We were singing a really heavy rock song about a sort of deer. The lyrics were incredibly inappropriate: "Hell's gazelle, bleeding meat between its teeth, its jaws were dripping with blood," or something.'

Just as Dan and Justin referenced their musical influences to create the band's sound, their East Anglian heritage provided lyrical inspiration. 'You can't deny where you come from,' Ed explained, 'a lot of rock bands try and write general global songs to try and appeal to everyone. But we try to be more honest.'

The mythology of the literal 'arse end of Britain' provided Justin with much source material. 'One of our songs ['Black Shuck'] is about an East Anglian hell hound with a red eye who attacked a church,' he recounted, 'we've got one about the Tollund Man; no-one knows anything about him, so we speculate what happened to him. I sort of say it's like the curse of the Egyptian pharaohs when they get dug up – the same sort of thing happened to the people that dug up the Tollund Man. Well, that's what I say in my song anyway.'

Whereas songs about the Tollund Man (an Iron Age victim of human sacrifice) and the ancient Saxon settlement/burial site of Sutton Hoo soon went the way of 'Hell's Gazelle', 'Black Shuck' remains part of the band's set to this day. Like Justin, Ed remembers being fascinated by the myth as a child. 'It's something we talked about in school, and if you see this dog, well, basically you don't want to see it because if you do see it, it means you and your family are all about to die, but this is like the black devil dog that walks around in the marshes with red eyes . . . . There was a church and in the middle ages it was said to have run in and the vicar held a cross up to it, so it ran out, but as it ran out it scratched the door and then the church was struck by lightning but you can see the door with the scratch marks in it!'

More prosaic, Justin's lyrics also drew upon 'matters of the heart' and memories of growing up in a provincial resort. Despite total conviction in his songwriting abilities – 'I do insist on writing all my own lyrics . . . I don't think I could do it if it was someone else writing them and they were bad' – Justin found the concept of social realism difficult to embrace. 'I tried to write about heroin addiction loads of times,' he admitted. 'I know people who have issues with that but it's difficult to write about if you're not the perpetrator.'

However, despite the chasm between the Darkness's emphasis on fun and the distinctly unfunny existence of the smack addict, Justin assimilated these mutually-exclusive elements to write 'Givin' Up' – which was deemed good enough to appear on their debut album. However, recordings and tours were distant ambitions at that stage. 'We know we've got a long struggle,' confessed Dan. 'No-one dares break any rules. But once we get unleashed, we could change everything.'

At 8.30pm on 12 August 2000, The Darkness made their full professional debut at the Monarch pub on Chalk Farm Road in Camden. The group had recently added an additional guitarist, Chris McDougal, who hooked up with them during their recent sessions, and the

Leeds believes in a thing called love, August 2003.

TV stars – The band prepare for their appearance on 'The Pop Factory', November 2002.

quintet pounded through their eight-song set in around half an hour. Although their performance was far removed from the polished show of three years hence, it was reviewed by the website *Musicunsigned* website as 'more glamorous than Shirley Bassey, but still every bit as timeless and relevant now as a million Coldplays.'

It was also good enough to convince the promoters of the Monarch's Barfly club to invite the band to return. These subsequent engagements (on 13 October and 18 November) saw the group experimenting with elements of indie and traditional rock, and even sea shanties. Despite the third gig providing their first headlining slot, some reassessment was still necessary. That Christmas and New Year period saw McDougal's departure. 'I wanted to play less guitar,' explained Justin, 'so we had a second guitarist. But, obviously, being something of a virtuoso when it comes to guitar playing, I'd listen to this bloke play his solos and think he was nowhere as good as me. So I took over that too.'

Guided by Sue Whitehouse, the group set up their own website, compiled a promotional mailing list and designed a series of eye-catching flyers for their gigs. The value of such support was not lost on Frankie: 'Having management makes a huge difference. It's being part of a great team and growing together. You don't have to be great players or be an expert producer – it's just about growing and developing together. It's important to get someone on-board who's on your side early on and someone who already has relationships with the music industry.'

The Darkness's return to the Monarch, on 1 March 2001, provided (despite some sound problems) a solid platform from which to relaunch their bid for global conquest.

Initially, the Monarch could lay claim to being the band's live 'home'. As Dan recalled, 'We only had one place that would book us so we played there every Saturday of the month for six months. It became a bit of a residency. That's something I'd say to bands – you don't always

Looning in loons – Frankie, Ed, Justin and Dan.

Dan, Frankie and Ed pause for reflection during an interview, Reading, August 2003.

When we started off it was high impact and some fairly dodgy costumes and songs. It took a year to sound exciting and rocking and another to sound crafted and have good songs. **Dan Hawkins**

have to go all round the country and play loads of venues to get a decent following – in fact if you play one venue again and again then people know where to see you and what to expect.'

The group saw the Barfly residency as an opportunity to develop their live act, whilst attempting to attract a regular audience. Given the pitfalls of learning in public, it was shrewdly decided they should confine their shows to the weekend, in the hope of avoiding corporate attention. 'We didn't really want to grow up under the industry's eye, so originally we were only going to do gigs on the weekend, 'cos we know that you'll get all the A&R men out mid-week,' justified Justin.

Occasional excursions to the Verge in Kentish Town and the Water Rats pub at Kings Cross filled in blank dates between Barfly engagements, as the band accumulated experience and confidence. Although Frankie Poullain recalls the earliest Darkness gigs as 'sporadic shows that were met with largely derision,' the group had begun to attract a hardcore following. 'Word spread through our website,' remembers Frankie. 'There would be information about our gigs and we'd get mentions on other people's sites. We had a big e-mail list we sent flyers out to. Everything just snowballed and eventually we developed enough of a following to make people sit up and take notice.'

Having acquired an audience, The Darkness duly set about ensuring that they were entertained. As befits a band who draw upon the bravura stadium rock of Queen and AC/DC, they quickly developed very specific ideas about their performances. 'When you play live you've got two choices, you can either be a band that stands at the back of the stage near your amp where it sounds good, or you can get into it and stand right at the front, put on a show and really connect with the crowd,' Dan asserted.

'A good live show is about having confidence in what you're doing and getting that across to the audience,' observed Frankie. 'It's basically about having good songs, a flamboyant front man, a tight rhythm section and balls of steel. You have to be a version of yourself. If you think of a writer for example, they create characters, which are often biographical myths of themselves. It's similar for a singer. As a lead singer you're projecting a version of yourself.'

As The Darkness's sound and image began to come together, the band established an ethos based on tight musicianship and a determination to give the punters a good night out. On 5 May, they took things a step further by laying on a buffet tea. 'I almost cut my finger off, making cheese cubes,' recalled Dan.

'That was Ed's idea. We chipped in £10 each, and made it ourselves,' Justin added. 'It started because he eats sandwiches off his drum kit. We call it a Snare Buffet.' Such hospitality, combined with their distinctly untrendy rock music, and Justin's unreconstructed capering, led to the band being dismissed by some observers as a novelty act.

Justin, however, had little time for such criticism. 'All we know is what we were brought up with and what we like. It's important to be fulfilled in what you're doing, and you won't get that if you're copying someone else or trying to fit the current trend. I've seen bands go from being Blur to Oasis in the space of a fortnight. That isn't fair to your audience, and you can lose people by not believing in what you're doing.'

The group's refusal to abandon the Good Ship Rock, despite the prevailing indie tide, was also dismissed by Frankie. 'The difference with rock is that it's all about working hard, playing hard and showing discipline. Indie bands don't have the ability to do any of that.'

'Playing live is all about living each day blind and pushing it to the limit,' announced Justin. 'There are people who compare us to the likes of Thin Lizzy and Queen and they say it in a way like "that's a bad thing" – you're talking about world beating, classic bands with people all over the world that absolutely love them. To me it's a coolness thing really. I personally haven't got any time for anybody who sees it as anything other than a good band.'

'You can tell the bands who are too over-the-top because they don't have good songs,' added Dan. 'Bands like KISS and Poison over-iced the cake, they had no real backbone; whereas bands like AC/DC and Queen and a lot of classic British rock bands really had that musicianship, too.'

'The genre that we're operating in is funny,' Justin observed. 'You know, in the eighties, everybody used to laugh at bands like Europe and Mötley Crüe, but they knew that themselves. There's that video of Mötley Crüe, where they've got the big hair and they're spraying hairspray around . . . I'm sure they must have known.'

In addition to supplying the faithful with a slap-up supper, The Darkness's Kentish Town gig provided the band with their first national press exposure. In an *Independent on Sunday* review, Simon Price became the first national journalist to recognise the stirrings of greatness: 'As yet unsigned, but creating quite a buzz, The Darkness – a histrionic, high camp heavy metal band – have a recurring gimmick: setting up a buffet table and offering tea and cake to their ever-growing cult audience. It's not the only incongruity about a band who are best described as a gay AC/DC fronted by a young Freddie Mercury. Terrible name notwithstanding, The Darkness are hugely entertaining, regardless of their exact location on the irony-seriousness scale.'

Favourable reviews also began to appear throughout the electronic media, with Pippa Moye's *Musicomh* article paying fulsome tribute: 'The set ranged from power ballads to camp rock pastiche. Fancy guitar-work and melodramatic poses were delicately balanced on solid riffs. The Darkness lamented life's cruel moments and celebrated silliness. Their songs possessed soul, sentiment and cunning clichés, delivered with ludicrous overstatement and crafty musicianship. Essence of the Stones, Thin Lizzy and AC/DC was captured in The Darkness' home-grown neo-classic anthems.'

This show, at the Monarch on 14 July, also introduced Justin's end-of-gig 'walkabout', usually perched upon the shoulders of soundman Pedro Ferreira. It was an obvious AC/DC reference – they originated the practice in the 1970s, with Angus Young transported hither and yon by the mighty Bon Scott. Justin is quick to identify the influence of the antipodean legends, acknowledging how, 'AC/DC have provided years of inspiration.' Dan is similarly respectful. 'You're not going to get much better than them live, are you? We saw them last year, and they've still got it. They're these blokes with thinning hair in their fifties or whatever, and in the first five minutes they sweated so much it was like they were about eighteen again.

People kept telling us to tone it down. But, if anything, that made us go the opposite way. If someone suggested Frankie trimmed his moustache, he'd grow it longer. **Dan Hawkins**

The next step forward for the band came with their 2 November show at the Underworld in Camden. Although still encumbered by presenting their grandiose glam within the smallest of venues, it represented a definite move up the live circuit's totem pole. The past eight months were beginning to reap dividends – they now had a recognisably distinctive set and a cohesive stage act. Justin had been working hard on his star-jumps and handstands which, combined with his musical histrionics, made him impossible to ignore.

The band had already written such future hits as 'I Believe In A Thing Called Love', and had even secured a degree of sponsorship from Mesa Boogie amplifiers. It all served to endow them with a newfound confidence, more than evident in the performance they set before the near-capacity crowd. For the first time, the band were playing before a sizeable mosh-pit of their own making.

Having already described The Darkness as 'The most overblown, vainglorious, vital band ever to have placed foot upon monitor,' *The Fly* fanzine reviewed the Underworld outing in a similar enthusiastic vein. Focusing on Justin's showmanship, journalist Matt Everitt observed, 'Possessed of a phenomenal voice (part Bon Scott, part Freddie Mercury and part Luciano Pavarotti) he preened and posed through the belting stadium rock, riff heavy melodies of "Nothing's Gonna Stop Us" and "Live 'Til I Die" with lung busting rock operatic charisma and panache, while his three fellow Darknessians plunged and powered with DC licks and driving rhythms.'

A fortnight after the triumphant Underworld showcase, The Darkness undertook two bold

Justin's furry trousers meet their Waterloo – supporting The Disturbed at Brixton Academy, December 2002.

Justin at Knebworth, submitting to a rigorous pre-show routine of champagne gargling, August 2003.

steps that would be embroidered into the band's mythos. Firstly, they made their debut outside the Camden/Kentish Town/Kings Cross triangle. Their initial south London splashdown was booked for 'Wolfie's Jukebox', in the back room of the Castle pub on Tooting High Street. Prior to The Darkness, the venue's most notable live gigs had been in the late 1970s, with local punks the UK Subs and all-girl rock combo Girlschool. But the night of 10 November saw The Darkness make their mark on Tooting's rich rock heritage.

Although greeted by a modest turn-out, Justin chose this occasion to inaugurate his legendary catsuit. The garment was unfurled mid-set, and, after minutes of grunting and straining, with two helpful onlookers assisting in the removal of his trousers, the nascent rock god stood resplendent before the gathered masses (or the gathered several).

'Image is important,' offered Justin. 'I much prefer to see a band with a bloke in a catsuit than someone standing there in jeans and T-shirt like they've just walked off a bus. You have to be prepared to entertain people.'

The snug-fitting world of catsuits had been opened up to Justin by his mother. 'I was looking on the net for interesting stage costumes and I remembered my mum telling me about being in this club and [Rolling Stone] Brian Jones – who she had a bit of a fancy to – turned up in this pink catsuit.' On researching the subject further, the vocalist discovered both a new sartorial direction and that 'there's a lot of fetish sites out there!'

Whilst not everyone in the band was convinced of the entertainment value of a catsuit, a new red number was unfurled at the Notting Hill Arts Club a fortnight later. Back on the safe side of the Thames, the show had been arranged by Sue Whitehouse in conjunction with club organiser Ian Johnsen, who was also the co-founder of Must Destroy Records. Johnsen had first seen the band at the Monarch earlier that year, and had been immediately impressed: 'They came on and me and my girlfriend stood with our jaws on the floor. We couldn't stop talking about them afterwards.'

Prior to the Notting Hill gig, there had been little music industry interest in the band. As Frankie recalled, 'We had lots of A&R people walking out after two songs. Of course, what was totally ridiculous and laughable then is now genius.'

But the Notting Hill show was attended by booking agent Rad Saunders, who was impressed enough to request a meeting with the band and refused to leave until they agreed he would act on their behalf.

Before breaking for the festive season, the group rounded off the year with a pair of shows at the Water Rats and the Monarch. Although the latter gig was plagued by a poor turn-out and dodgy sound, the contrast with the final days of Empire – just a year earlier – could hardly have been more marked. Whereas Dan and Justin had seen out the previous year contemplating whether to abandon their rock ambitions, December 2001 saw them with a small but growing following that numbered around 200 'Darklings'.

The band had put together the basis of a storming live show, and, whilst A&R people prevaricated over whether the band were ironic, post-ironic or simply having a laugh, interest seemed to be growing with every gig. As far as Justin was concerned, any talk of irony was beside the point. 'Our basic motivation when we play is to make sure everyone in the room watching us is having a good time. And there's a lot of different prongs to our attack; the performance is one part, the costumes are another, the tightness of songwriting. And that's not ridiculous. There's not many bands pushing things to the extreme that we do, but I've never thought of us as ridiculous.'

I can confirm that there is nothing freakish about my genitalia. Justin Hawkins

'Outrageous maybe,' added Dan, 'but never ridiculous.'

Having spent the past twelve months polishing his showmanship as much as his solos, Justin remained staunchly devoted to his catsuits. If the band were to become stadium behemoths, then their front man was going to dress appropriately. 'I've always yearned to be able to perform onstage in a catsuit,' he confirmed. 'In a way I think it was probably Rod Stewart or perhaps Freddie [Mercury], although he's only been a more recent influence to me. I just loved the idea of dressing in a catsuit. I've been going to see bands for like thirteen, fourteen years, and I've yet to see anyone come onstage wearing a Lycra catsuit. It just really works for me.'

However, given the flimsiness of some of his earliest suits, Justin readily admitted the concept was still a work-in-progress. 'I had tried it previously but more cheaply and contacted a dance studio that did rehearsal uniforms and they custom made something for me. But they'd just stuck together some cheap Lycra and my balls were hanging out everywhere. It just went all wrong. They then gave me a jockstrap which was flesh coloured to wear with it, to try and keep it all in, but it just didn't cut it. People just didn't know where to look. It was embarrassing for a lot of people, not for me because I was really feeling good in it.'

Regardless of how camp the suits made him look, or how regularly his bollocks came to prominence, there was no denying that such flamboyance drew attention. 'There's no finer sight than me stumbling around a backstage corridor in my catsuit with a bottle of vodka in my hand,' insisted Justin.

09

3

Darkness Rising

Cock rock is our calling. For years, people didn't even dignify it with a reaction. It was more like, if we ignore it, maybe it'll go away. But you know, now it's back – and it's wearing shorts. **Justin Hawkins**

The New Year started on a bright note for The Darkness, when their policy of mailing out demo-tapes paid off with a wholehearted review on the website *tipsheet.co.uk*. The anthemic 'Love Is Only A Feeling' was awarded 'Demo of the Week' status, whilst their re-tooling of stadium rock was roundly praised: 'the sound is heavily influenced by seventies and eighties classic rock, but it works because they do it with 21st century production, because no-one else has sounded like this for a while, and because they do it so unashamedly.'

Other recipients of the tape included the organisers of the South by Southwest festival – an annual new-music showcase based in Austin, Texas. In exchange for their submission and a $20 registration fee, the band were delighted to receive an invitation to appear along with this enthusiastic response: 'Just wanted to drop you a line to tell you The Darkness CD is my favourite thing that's come into the SXSW offices this year, out of 5,000 submissions. I've played it to lots of people. My friend John Darnielle (who performs as the Mountain Goats) said, "This shit is immortal!" Rock the fuck on!'

'That was pretty refreshing,' said Justin, 'especially when they invited us over and paid for

Justin wins over Robbie's thousands at Knebworth.

our accommodation.' Despite The Darkness never having travelled south of the River Wandle, let alone the Mason-Dixon line, Justin was unwavering in his conviction. 'Rock is a nation in itself, it transcends international boundaries. And we're setting our sights further than Britain.'

The band warmed up for their US 'mini-tour' by sandwiching a show for family and friends in Cambridge and an intrepid excursion to Sheffield between dates in Kentish Town and Camden. Their 6 February show at the Monarch saw two new numbers added to the growing set, 'Where Do I Stand?' and 'Makin' Out'.

Just over a month later, on 15 March, The Darkness made their US debut before an 11 am full house at Maggie Mae's in Austin. In his review for the website *playlouder.com*, festival attendee Andy Barding was much taken with the band's traditional British reserve: 'Visiting Dutch and Belgian delegates watch in mortified awe as our man scissor kicks his way through such unlikely delights as an acoustic 'How Dare You Call This Love?' Justin stalks the huge hall to personally serenade the badge-clad bores who are trying to guzzle down their breakfast, the faithful are clapping along in devilish Whitesnake fashion to "Love Is Only A Feeling".'

Despite this early triumph, the downside of transatlantic touring became evident. For one thing the costs incurred in transporting their equipment stretched the band's spandex purse to breaking point. But, if lack of funds was an inconvenience during the tour, when Justin and Sue's relationship finally came to light it unexpectedly blew up in their faces.

For Dan, Frankie and Ed, the discovery that their vocalist and manager were engaged, and that their liaison had been kept from them, was deeply unsettling. Likewise, the stress of keeping the whole situation quiet for two years, and then being exposed, suddenly placed an emotional burden on Sue and Justin.

'We wondered if people would approve of us going out, because she's been managing me and my brother Dan for seven years, so we kept it secret,' explained Justin. 'It was like we were having an illicit affair but it was just two people getting together. We fell in love – she is the best manager in the business.'

This particular bombshell led to a frank exchange of opinions. It was the closest the band have

Frankie makes some final backstage adjustments, MTV2 5th Birthday concert, September 2003.

Justin giving his all at the Hammersmith Apollo.

Supported by the sturdy Pedro Ferreira, Justin embarks upon another 'walkabout', February 2003.

ever been to splitting up. 'The shit really hit the fan,' observed Justin. 'They wanted to sack her because we got together. And I said if you sack her, you sack me, so none of us got sacked.'

'It got pretty emotional,' confirmed Frankie, 'lots of stuff was said that shouldn't have been said.' Once the dust had settled, however, common sense held sway. There was never the slightest question concerning Sue's commitment to The Darkness. She had worked tirelessly for the collective whole, and for each individual member. In keeping the relationship a secret, she and Justin had done the wrong thing for the right reasons. There was no cynicism behind the secrecy, and certainly no doubting the strength of Justin's feelings. 'We are engaged,' he confirmed. 'I bought her a lovely ring when it was a secret – it was a romantic gesture, every penny I had went on it. At that time we were just going to go off and get married and then tell everyone we were together. That would have been superb, but then everyone found out about it.'

With frayed tempers back under control, The Darkness wrapped up their American mini-odyssey with a show at the Roxy on West Sunset Boulevard, Hollywood. Before another full house, they blasted out an energised set and drew an

I consider myself an unknown hero, so the longer we stay an unknown band the better. I have an evil plot where I'll go from being an unknown no-hoper to an evil genius and that'll be it – no in between. It'll be overnight, I'll wake up one morning, and there you go. **Justin Hawkins**

enthusiastic response. Justin was in fine form – resplendent in furry flares, the master of subtle understatement wowed onlookers with gravity-defying star-jumps from the top of the speaker stacks.

'This is what I've always wanted to do – conquer America,' enthused Dan. Even being billed as 'The Darkenss' failed to diminish his delight. Such overstatement was typical, but

Justin salutes the Brixton throng, February 2003.

returning to London provided the band with a melancholic sense of perspective. As Justin put it, in unusually downbeat mode, 'I didn't plan on coming back to England, because nothing was really happening for us in the UK. We thought we would spend the rest of our lives kicking it up on the Sunset Strip, but it didn't happen.'

Although the dates in Austin and LA had allowed the band to indulge their fantasies, the sharp-focus reality was that they were broke, unsigned, and would need to funnel any profits from their next three gigs into keeping their clapped-out Volkswagen camper on the road. To put the tin hat on everything, Dan had managed to throw most of his clothes out with the rubbish. Twice.

A timely dose of light relief was provided by the band's newly-recruited costume designer, Nancy. Recruited by Sue via an advertisement in *Music Week*, Nancy had enraptured the group with her cheery disposition and grand tales of styling the Luxembourg royal family. Conceptually, the stylist had her own unique ideas about the quartet's visual image.

'She said she saw me as a wizard, Justin as the Beast Master, Frank as a dandy and Ed as . . . It might have been Flash Gordon,' revealed Dan. 'We went along with it until Nancy turned up with the costumes before one of our biggest gigs at Ocean in Hackney around April Fools Day. My wizard costume was a massive cloak, which stretched out either side like a giant bell with owl feathers around the collar, which made me look like Henry VIII. Ed had a black sleeveless t-shirt with enormous silver Flash Gordon shoulder pads. Frank had a dark

We're quite tough, that's what makes us the band we are. Apart from the talent factor, we're durable people, not flaky indie kids. **Frankie Poullain**

Edwardian jacket with a rubber snake sewn around the lapels. Only Justin was happy in his Beast Master trousers with a long fox tail belt and fluffy shin pads. We haven't seen her since.'

'We knew it wasn't right at the time,' understated Ed, 'but then none of us said anything.'

The Hackney concert was followed by shows in Kentish Town and Cardiff. With the profits from all three gigs providing the Darkness-mobile with a new tax disc, the band were able to fulfil agent Rad Saunders' policy of wider exposure. One such excursion took the band to the Varsity in Wolverhampton, on 11 June. Although the gig drew no more than a handful of thrill-seekers, it was to provide The Darkness with their biggest break so far.

Known for exploring the grassroots of contemporary popular culture, *Dazed and Confused* had elected to cover the show as part of a feature on the travails of a struggling rock band. In terms of producing good copy, they could hardly have picked a better night. The Darkness were not having the best of days – their van had partially disentegrated *en route* and Frankie's bass fell from its stand, leaving him stuck with a junior-sized replacement.

Dazed and Confused's Rowan Chernin described a moment of pure Spinal Tap tragicomedy that has since passed into Darkness folklore: '"I dedicate this next song to you five," shouts Justin, "you know who you are." A mobile phone starts ringing, the second one this show. Justin looks around as the rest of the band pretend they can't hear anything. "For fuck's sake Frank, answer that fucking phone." "Hello Mum, I'm on stage," says Frank casually. "FFFFF-FUUUUUCK," screams Justin.'

The day ended as badly as it had begun, when, after the long drive back to London, the group were unable to get into their lock-up to stash their equipment for the night. But, as

Justin enjoys some backstage hospitality at the Brixton Academy, September 2003.

ever, Justin remained undaunted. 'Already we're kind of legendary in some quarters,' he affirmed, 'because we're flying a flag no one has flown for a long time.'

For The Darkness, tomorrow was indeed another day. The following evening saw the band closer to home ground, at the Metro on Oxford Street. The previous evening's disappointments were washed away on a tide of high spirits (at extortionate West End prices). Greeted by an enthusiastic crowd of old faces and curious sensation-seekers, the band put in a storming set that made up for the Wolverhampton debacle.

Once the sumptuous twelve-page spread accorded to the band by *Dazed and Confused* hit the shelves, however, even the Wolvehampton trip could be viewed as a success. Not only was it an unprecedented level of coverage for an unsigned band, but it provided The Darkness's collective profile with an enormous boost.

'We're reintroducing the rock genre to people who were never into that music before,' announced Justin. '*Dazed and Confused* gave us about ten pages for style kids who have never been to a rock gig.'

However, despite the welcome exposure, the tone of the piece strayed a little too close to *Spinal Tap* territory for Justin's comfort. 'At the time they were doing a run of issues where the main features were completely unheard of. They had a photographer a couple of months before that issue who went on to do great things from then on. It was their opportunity to spot folk. It gave us a leg up really and it was nice of them to do it, but they did go in a bit hard on the loser angle, which wasn't funny at the time.'

'People have misconceptions,' added Frankie, clearly in two minds about it. 'All this stuff about style mags being interested in us, it was our one and only piece and it wasn't even a fashion piece.'

After a one-off excursion to Cardiff, the quartet's next two London gigs, at the Water Rats and

Dan and Justin lead the handclaps at Brixton, February 2003.

the Hackney Ocean on 11 and 12 July, were attended by a higher proportion of A&R reps and music journalists than previously. Whether specific individuals had gone to see the band out of genuine interest or to gawp at the 'losers' was largely irrelevant – The Darkness were being noticed.

Resplendent in his furry flares, Justin was the inevitable centre of attention – as *Honk* fanzine's review of the Cardiff show made plain: 'He shimmies and cavorts like Mick Jagger, star jumping and leaping like an old pro. He plays guitar behind his head. He comes down offstage into the audience and continues his heavy-rock falsetto hybrid. This lot are a brilliant headache – there's simply no one else like them at the moment. Who else could get away with a bassist with a Freddie Mercury moustache? It's about time pop rock became cool again.'

Despite the growing hullabaloo, the absence of any concrete offers from record labels prompted Sue Whitehouse to seize the initiative. Aware that Ian Johnsen had recently set up the Must Destroy label with co-founder Alan Hake, she sounded him out about the possibility of releasing a Darkness single.

One of Johnsen's reasons for starting the label was to put out music by bands that larger companies had overlooked, and his earlier involvement had left him with a favourable impression. 'The first time I saw The Darkness, two years ago, they were a fully-formed stadium rock band that happened not to be playing stadiums,' he asserted.

Although no contracts were signed, the band were booked into the 2KHz Studios on Scrubs Lane, north west London. Once in the studio, the band recorded three live anthems – 'I Believe In A Thing Called Love', 'Love On The Rocks With No Ice' and 'Love Is Only A Feeling'. Stereophonics producer Pedro Ferreira was installed at the mixing desk, ensuring that the abundant majesty of the band's live show made a successful transition. Surprisingly, Justin opted to dispense with such essentials as catsuits and furry loons during the recording process. 'I like to record starkers,' he explained helpfully. 'When I'm in the studio I like to express myself more freely – I guess I'm an exhibitionist.' No wonder the EP was almost too sexy for public release . . .

The *I Believe In A Thing Called Love* EP was released through Must Destroy on 12 August 2002. It arrived hot on the heels of three Darkness shows in Glasgow (an AC/DC tribute night), Sheffield and Camden. Given that it was confined to an initial pressing of 2,000 copies, it was hardly surprising that it made little impact on the UK chart. Although the disc was re-pressed on two occasions, the total number was still small enough to ensure that copies now regularly change hands for in excess of £70.

Far more significant was the increased level of exposure resulting from their first release. The 17 August issue of *Kerrang!* featured the band twice – Dan and Justin were interviewed by Dave Everley for the regular 'Rising' feature, and 'I Believe' was made Single of the Week.

Pitted against a selection of re-heated ska-punk, dodgy nu-metal and self-indulgent angst-rock, it's easy to see why The Darkness's debut stuck out like an elephant's ears. Reviewer Paul Travis instantly recognised the group's over-inflated brilliance: 'It starts with a riff lifted straight from KISS, circa "Crazy Crazy Nights". Then the vocals kick in and the first thought that strikes you is that it must be a joke. A Tenacious D-type affair perhaps, or someone semi-famous having a lark around. It's a warbling falsetto, you see, so wonderfully, gloriously over the top it makes Muse's Matt Bellamy sound like Lemmy farting through cheesecloth. Add guitars that revel unashamedly in the majesty of rock, a trio of deliciously overblown song titles and you have a single that is so utterly preposterous it can only be the work of genius.'

The *Playlouder.com* website was equally enthusiastic, asserting that The Darkness were no gimmick: 'we are becoming increasingly convinced that there is no irony involved here, as the band have the songs, the live show and the balls to get them massive success.'

Frankie, Justin, Ed and Dan at the MTV2 5th Birthday concert, September 2003.

NME were also positive – but oddly confused in terms of Justin's sexuality, and that of rockers in general: 'Imagine if Jon Bon Jovi sang like his trousers were cutting off the circulation to his scrotum. You're some way to understanding the bombastic appeal of London's The Darkness – rock reanimators with a difference. And that difference is operatic singer Justin Hawkins, a man who, like any real rock beast, prefers men to girls. The power of his falsetto is felt most keenly on "Love On The Rocks With No Ice", a song so overblown, so perfect, you may as well give in to the eighties poodle metal revival now.'

Considering the resolutely desolate nature of rock music at the time, any band predominantly concerned with having a good time would be met by mixed feelings. Stadium rock had long been viewed as little more than a parody genre. Only AC/DC had successfully managed to rise above the howls of derision in much the same manner as they survived the near-obliteration of good-time metal during punk's apocalyptic heyday.

However, there were signs that the climate was changing – earlier in the year, a minor media storm had developed around the release of ultra-positive fun rocker Andrew WK's debut release, and the emergence of a number of excellent garage rock bands like the Datsuns, the D4 and Jet demonstrated that something resembling old-school rock was once again on the menu. As far as The Darkness were concerned, any debate as to whether the band were 'taking the piss out of rock' was beside the point. As Dan told *Kerrang!*, 'It scares people that we really don't give a shit. People can laugh all they want. They'll be forced to take us seriously eventually.'

Are we 'the gay AC/DC'? I prefer 'the straight Queen'! **Dan Hawkins**

As the summer wore on, the growing debate about the band crossed over from the music press to the national papers. The *Guardian Guide* identified The Darkness as 'leaders, pretty much, in a field of one,' whilst *The Independent*'s Steve Jelbert was less faint with his praise: 'The Darkness are single-handedly attempting to rehabilitate eighties hair metal in a country with no basketball arenas to perform in. The singer/guitarist Justin (his name is tattooed on his shoulder, with a lightning bolt replacing the "s"), may be to David Lee Roth what Dick Van Dyke was to Cockneys, but as he sprints around a tiny pub, a radio mike on his "axe", clad in somewhat threadbare velvet hipsters, you have to set aside any thoughts of sniggering.'

The key to The Darkness lay in comprehending the distinction between fun and outright comedy. The band were far too musically accomplished, and had devoted too much time to refining their sound and image, to be dismissed as a novelty act. 'Obviously we don't see ourselves as cheesy or we wouldn't be wasting all this time working really fucking hard to fight against the grain,' asserted Frankie.

Reviewing the band's 14 August Notting Hill Arts Club concert, journalist Stevie Chick hit the nail on the head: 'This is rock 'n' roll as escape from dull reality, not some grey dreary reflection thereof.' Reassuringly, there were plenty of people who *did* get The Darkness, notably Radio One DJ Jo Whiley – who installed 'I Believe' as her single of the week. 'People were craving some real entertainment, with stars who put on a real performance, after too many years of bland pop stars being thrown at us,' expounded Whiley. 'People now want to have a laugh, without trying to be outrageously cool the whole time.'

Having taken to the road in support of their single, The Darkness set about broadening their fan base through the sheer spandex grandeur of their live show. Although audience response became progressively more fervent with each gig, press reaction remained fixated on

The Legion of Rock Superheroes surveys the capital from the London Eye, April 2003.

The Darkness's credibility, or lack thereof.

In his *Guardian* review of the group's 6 September concert at the Metro, long-time supporter Simon Price railed against this. 'We're now so attuned to assuming that a band who raise smiles must have some sort of kitsch agenda that we've forgotten how to enjoy ourselves,' Price observed. 'The Darkness are, in every sense, a scream. They're funny, all right: Justin Hawkins, with his Freddie Mercury falsetto, David Lee Roth gymnastics and mid-song stunts knows all about entertainment. But a genuine, unfakeable love of this music (think AC/DC, Thin Lizzy, think AC/DC again) shines through.'

Likewise, a review of the same show on the website *thestereoeffect.com* identified the good time appeal of the quartet: 'any potential to descend into camp *Spinal Tap* parody is given a cowboy-booted kick up its ass by the sheer head-down, ball-bustin' boogie of the songs.'

Whereas the tone of these reviews was overwhelmingly positive, some *NME* hacks took a more dismissive attitude. 'They said the only darkness we should see is if a real musician puts a bag over our heads and suffocates us,' explained Ed.

'That's because they can't believe it,' asserted Dan. 'I think people find it hard to believe what they're actually seeing. They think there's some kind of ironic master plan behind it but there isn't. We're just doing what we really like doing.'

NME had failed to get to grips with the idea that, just because a band don't take themselves too seriously, it doesn't necessarily indicate that they're a joke. The superficiality irritated Justin. 'The *NME* reviewed our live show and it was a real slag-off. They were talking about me having shit teeth, and they were talking about everything apart from the music, really.'

Despite this, the band were were not going to take such criticism seriously. 'We've all been in bands before and the lesson we've learnt is that you have to be yourself, you have to do what

You want to project a bit of fun in your image. Dan Hawkins

Justin comes over all Dave Lee Roth, in LA, September 2003.

'Rrring me. . . .' Justin in his love pit.

you like otherwise what you do is going to be watered down. For our pains we're equally reviled and loved but that's great,' observed Frankie. 'Secretly they don't know what they're hating. That kind of hate can turn to love. It's the same as when you're with a lady, like the Clark Gable kind of movies where the woman hits him but she really loves him. The *NME* will sleep with us eventually. They'll probably have to do it against our will, they'll probably have to rape us!'

As an explanation of his magazine's snotty *hauteur*, former *NME* editor Conor McNicholas offered, 'The music doesn't do anything for me, but I respect what they do. I don't think it has legs unless they do something to move it on. They are just living out their fantasies by replaying their favourite bands, but they need to bring some meaning to it.'

It seems fair enough, but the insistence that all entertainment should be imbued with 'meaning' underlines precisely why McNicholas and his staff so spectacularly missed the point.

Although *NME* may have hoped The Darkness would stop wasting their time with hair-metal frivolities, there was no shortage of critics who simply enjoyed the band at face value. Realising how Justin and chums were not so much breathing new life into the bloated corpse of stadium rock as sticking their tongues down its throat and waking it up with a boner, *The*

The Darkness get cosy in Old Glory, September 2003.

Independent's Steve Jelbert predicted the band would be 'bigger than a footballer's house'. *Kerrang!*, as befits its rock-fundamentalist roots, was unwavering in it support of the group, describing them as 'the greatest British rock 'n' roll band of the last twenty years'. 'They are shameless,' explained former editor-in-chief Phil Alexander. 'They represent the good times of rock 'n' roll. They're the antidote to the miserablism we've experienced in music for so long. They're saying, "Life is there to be lived, have a great time."'

'We are real fuckin' rock,' agreed Dan. 'We're not taking it lightly. But also we realise the most pretentious thing you can do is take yourself too seriously.'

'Perhaps there's a misconception among some people that what we do is contrived, but there is no masterplan,' explained Frankie. 'Justin is not some kind of evil Svengali. The first time he did a headstand on stage, he did it to amuse himself and us. Our number one thing

The British are coming! The band touch down in Los Angeles, September 2003.

HOLLYWOOD

ROXY

Justin shows off his dexterity to the Leeds Festival crowd, August, 2003.

People say we'll be gone in six months, but we'll be conquering Andorra by then. **Dan Hawkins**

from day one has been to turn the crowd on, to stop people from being cool and self-conscious.'

As ever, Justin remained resolute in his conviction that the strength of the band's material, along with the excitement of The Darkness's live show, would ensure success. 'We've got the ability to connect with people. Some bands are selfish, but we give the people what they want. They just don't know it yet.'

The band connected in the right way on 15 September, when they carried off the coveted Best Unsigned Band award at the annual 'In The City' music conference. The category had been previously won by Coldplay and Idlewild, and was seen as a passport to greater things. As with any industry event, the Salford show was packed with A&R people, press, and laminated-badge wearers of all stripes.

The Darkness put in a storming set, bolstered by the inclusion of a new song, 'Get Your Hands Off My Woman', collected their prize, and sat back to await the distinctive sound of swooping major labels. Incredibly, the anticipated interest failed to materialise. 'There were loads of people in the industry who loved the band but wouldn't sign them as it would probably mean they would risk losing credibility with their bosses,' Ian Johnsen recalled. 'It's easier for someone to sign a band from the New York scene, as that is cool and acceptable and won't look too bad if it goes wrong.'

To an extent, Justin understood the industry prevarication. 'People are initially shocked and think, "How can this be serious?" But if you come to a few gigs you realise it's not a joke, they're

Justin, Frankie, Dan and Ed outside The Roxy, Los Angeles, September 2003.

Thumbs across America – Justin onstage at The Roxy, LA, September 2003.

proper songs just delivered a different way. The bottom line is that we mean it.'

Although keen to secure a major contract, the band were more than satisfied with the support accorded them by Ian Johnsen and his Must Destroy label. Identified by Justin as part of The Darkness's 'kick-ass team who handle all the promotional stuff,' Johnsen was equally happy to continue his relationship with Lowestoft's finest. 'We put out their first single and got along with the band really well and we wanted to work with them more. Our distributor Vital said, "Yeah it's not something we'd normally do but we are willing to stick our hands in our pockets for this one."'

Whilst discussions ensued as to the band's next release, they were accorded the headline slot at the 'Best of In The City' showcase. Held on 25 September in the familiar environs of the Water Rats' back room, the show finished with the band performing a Queen medley comprised of 'Bohemian Rhapsody', 'Fat Bottomed Girls' and 'Crazy Little Thing Called Love'. It received an unequivocal 'five-K' review from *Kerrang!*'s Dave Everley: 'There's no doubting the fact that The Darkness will repel as many people as they attract because of the posturing, the preening, and the paint-peeling falsetto that propels their songs off the planet and out towards the third ring of Saturn. But it's this decoration, this air of flamboyant otherness that makes the band so great. And if you don't like it, then you've always got Puddle of Mudd.' The double-page *Kerrang!* spread featured a series of evocative images of Justin in his furry trousers (by now a little threadbare), throwing a series of classic rock shapes.

Most significantly, 'In The City' resulted in an invitation to support noted trad-rockers and human chemical dustbins the Wildhearts, on a short UK tour. Additionally, invites to appear at *Kerrang!*'s residential Weekender event arrived at Darkness HQ, alongside offers to perform sessions for Radio One and Xfm.

The Wildhearts support slot brought the band out of the pubs and into proper dancehalls, such as Dudley's JB's and the London Astoria. The headliners' fan base was receptive to The Darkness's fun-metal. Like northern rockers Terrorvision, the Wildhearts had spent much of the last decade ignoring current trends to pursue an infectious brand of rock accessibility. Although more denim-and-leather than spandex-and-sequin, they had more in common with The Darkness than the majority of other bands on the UK circuit.

It represented a golden opportunity for The Darkness to pick up converts, and Justin was in a determined mood: 'I think people have got to be sold to in the first five seconds. People seem shocked that we're actually there to provide a bit of entertainment, but by the end of the set they know they'll have heard some seriously good songs.'

With ample encouragement and support provided by Wildhearts mainstay Ginger ('They're like four real life David Lee Roths'), The Darkness, and Justin in particular, thrived on it all. 'We're starting to gather momentum. Being in the studio does put it all into perspective. Too much fucking perspective! The tour with the Wildhearts was a bit of an eye opener too – they're a zany group of characters. And certainly playing at the Astoria was great. I prefer being out on the road than in the studio. For the first week here I had nothing to do while they set up their instruments. Just sat here with my cock in my hand, at a bit of a loose end.'

It's men's rock with balls, and that never goes out. People either seem to like us or strongly hate us, but the balance of power is shifting, people in high places are beginning to appreciate The Darkness. Justin Hawkins

The expedition concluded with the *Kerrang!* event at Camber Sands, which provided a drunken outing for The Darkness's' five-a-side football team, as well as giving Justin the opportunity to DJ before a throng of horn-throwing holidaymakers.

After spending much of October working on material for a proposed album, the band headed for South Wales to shoot their television debut. The recording for HTV's *Pop Factory* saw the band rattle off thumping versions of 'I Believe In A Thing Called Love' and 'Black Shuck' – despite being hampered by the usual problems with Justin's genitals and his disentegrating stage wear.

Also appearing on the show were sub-Wheatus UK skater boys BBMak – who aroused Frankie's wrath by making off with his equipment. 'They were miming and wanted to borrow our drum kit and amps so they could try and look cool in front of all our Marshalls,' explained the bassist. '"Fine," I said. I went down to check their performance and stayed 30 seconds – long enough to realise that their "guitarist" had taken my capo and placed it on his guitar . . . this US multi-million selling band took my capo straight off stage into their gig bag into the back of their expensive people carrier and off to render another penniless musician short of the only money they have to eat that week. These capos are about £17 a go. I don't give a fuck if the guy likes us – he's gonna fucking get it big time, soon.'

But what the band had lost in kit was more than compensated for in terms of exposure. Proving an immediate hit with the audience, The Darkness were nominated for Best *Pop Factory* Performance and Best *Pop Factory* TV Debut awards. Although they lost out to Feeder and the Cooper Temple Clause in their respective categories, it ensured a return visit to the Porth studios.

Further exposure came in the first issue of Xfm Radio's companion magazine, *X-Ray*. Deeming them, 'Guilty of absolute bloody fabulousness,' *X-Ray* featured the band under the precipitous strap-line, 'Gonna Be Huge'. Certainly, Xfm programme director Andrew Phillips was convinced of the power of The Darkness: 'I think this band will reshape rock and make it fun again. There will always be those that will think it is a joke, but anyone with a realistic outlook on life will realise they have the fundamentals of what works as a song – something people can hum along to after it has finished playing. On the radio the songs get stronger and stronger. It's not just a music thing – they genuinely entertain which makes it a double whammy.'

With enough material for a debut album already in the can, The Darkness saw out 2002 with a series of eight gigs in a fortnight. In addition to describing Frankie Poullain as looking 'like a Dutch porn star', e-zine *rockfeedback.com* published a glowing account of the band's 27 November show at the Fez Club, Reading.

Subsequent dates at the Academy 3, Liverpool, and the redolently-named Empire, Middlesbrough, also attracted similar praise. Writing in the *Telegraph*, Neil McCormack observed, 'The Darkness have released only one single, yet, judging by the enthusiastic response in a packed venue, they may yet earn their own space in a future British Library exhibition.'

We've had to dig in at various times when the chips were down but we stuck through it. **Frankie Poullain**

The start of December saw the group's debut at the Brixton Academy, supporting 'Mad' Davey Draiman's lightweight nu-metal combo, the Disturbed. 'Their fans were a strange bunch,' recalled Justin. 'I think half of them despised us and the other half loved it. There was stuff being thrown at us and fights breaking out. We knew it would happen, we were expecting that kind of reaction from the start. But those bottles still hurt!'

Having survived sustained shelling by gloomy youths in hoodies, on 7 December the band made their first appearance at another bastion of metal, Rock City in Nottingham. A small show at Peterborough's Met Lounge prefaced the quartet's final show of the year, the Xfm Xmas Session at the newly relocated Marquee in Islington. Booked to support the seriously hip and regularly brilliant Libertines, The Darkness would have to be at their most sumptuous to squeeze any response from the throng of industry insiders, liggers and Libertines fundamentalists.

As the *Guardian* review described it, 'The crowd was made up in equal measure of self-consciously cool media types and slightly geeky sorts who looked as though they may have seen Whitesnake play Milton Keynes on more than one occasion. It took Justin Hawkins – the band's lithe, long-haired and lavishly tattooed front man – half an hour of headstands, star jumps and shrieking to work the diverse throng into a heaving mass of intoxicated disciples. Lifelong enemies of rock held their hands like devil's horns and raised them to the stage.'

The official festive posting on the official Darkness website observed, 'All in all, it's been a great year.' If anything, the webmaster was understating the case. Aside from the minor crisis in America, 2002 had seen the band's profile rise with each passing month. They started off playing in front of the Monarch faithful and ended up nominated by *Q*'s Paul Stokes as potentially 'the best new band in Britain'.

Behind the scenes, Sue Whitehouse had put together a closely orchestrated team comprising a promoter, a radio plugger and a PR agent to complement the support of Must Destroy and their distributors, Vital. Although delighted with the group's development, Justin was aware that, in order to progress further, feet needed to be kept firmly on the ground.

'We've already got a really strong following and although we haven't got the proper backing to do a proper fan club or anything,' he observed with practicality, 'we know who our fans are because I run the mailing list on the website. So everything goes through me and if anyone has an enquiry, or wants to meet us, then they do meet us. We don't fucking jet off in helicopters or anything, if there's something going on then we do it. We are a good time band and the main thing is we try and make sure they also have a good time. If they're having a good time then we're having a good time and that's our job.'

Or, as Frankie put it, more succinctly, 'We're being ourselves and keeping it real.'

The climactic 'walkabout' grinds to a halt at the Bowery Ballroom, New York, September 2003.

1-4 COMPS
5-8 GATES
9-12 GR.EQ
INSERTS

4

Adopting The Stance

We are the revolution and have been sent to pull rock from its own arsehole. **Frankie Poullain**

With the band's second single, 'Get Your Hands Off My Woman', scheduled for a late February release by Must Destroy, The Darkness began 2003 by shooting their first video. It was booked to take place at the Mean Fiddler in London's West End, on Sunday 19 January. Director John Sadler's appeal for extras had been posted on the official website. 'We need you to dress up and rock out!' it exalted. 'The most outrageously-dressed fans will feature more prominently in the final cut. Think glamorous, think leather, think cross-dressing, think groupies.'

Although legions of 'Darklings' responded magnificently, they never stood a chance of out-glamming Justin. The front man emerged in a new zebra-striped catsuit designed by the band's recently acquired costumier, Christian Hutter. His furry trousers now consigned to rock's great laundry basket, Justin was delighted to be prancing about in spandex again. 'It's what I feel comfortable in. It's the right thing to wear on stage. When I'm cooking I wear a cooking hat and if I'm presenting rock I present it in rock clothes.'

Having spent the early part of the day mixing with fans and DJ-ing, Justin took the stage to run through countless takes of the single. At the end of shooting, he pronounced himself more than satisfied: 'Everything's going swimmingly and I'm terribly excited by it all. I've seen a rough cut of the video, and it looks like a gig, which is mission accomplished I think. We're hoping to have a screening somewhere – a grand occasion with a lovely buffet with prawn sandwiches for the elite and what have you.'

The rock leopard emerges from the mist.

Aware that the high expletive count in 'Get Your Hands Off My Woman' was likely to ensure a complete absence of airplay, a 'radio-friendly' version was also recorded. 'I substituted the word "cunt" for "coconut" and "motherfucker" became "mummamumma" just mumbled into obscurity. It scans well so we're alright,' revealed Justin.

It doubtless delighted Ma Hawkins, who, whilst recognising the lyrics were 'rude, but they seem to fit,' reassured nervous Radio One listeners that if either offspring were to indulge in such potty talk at home, 'I'd knock their heads together.'

Although he described the number as 'one of the hardest of our songs to sing, all screaming,' Justin had no quibble with its selection as a single. 'This was a well chosen song for us to do I think, although next time it'll just be a simple dramatic monologue with me sitting on a stool. That could work quite well!'

Ahead of the single's release, The Darkness returned to live action with their first major support tour – backing veteran British rock heavyweights Def Leppard on a nine-date jaunt. The prospect of being on the road with the legendary Sheffield hair-metallers delighted Justin: 'We wanted to do it because the Sheffield Arena was one of the dates. Because we're an arena band. I'm expecting to be guided gently through the pitfalls of stadium rock by Joe Elliot and friends. I should think that most people will turn up after we've finished, but if we make a few friends it's a bonus!'

The tour opened at the Newport Centre in South Wales, on 15 February. Despite going down well, things got off on the wrong foot when Justin broke his toe during the post-gig knees-up. Although reportedly 'hopping mad', the limping lead vocalist got off lightly in comparison with Frankie's bass – which sustained a broken neck. 'I have to inch along very gently on my heels,' Justin explained.

Aside from some minor testicular damage caused by sliding down an iron girder, Ma Hawkins' eldest hobbled through the rest of the tour without suffering further injury. As well as making an impact on their dressing room, the band left a distinct impression on Def Leppard vocalist Elliot: 'They know what they're doing isn't Shakespeare, but it is different to anything else around and that is the true value. I remember when I first saw them supporting us in Newport, it was like watching AC/DC meets Queen fronted by the singer from Sparks. It is the start of a new generation of fun music, but it needs to be allowed to grow.'

The Darkness's 24 February debut at Glasgow's Barrowlands coincided with the release of their second single. Pressed as a three track EP, *Get Your Hands Off My Woman* featured both the original and 'clean' versions of the title track, alongside an established live favourite, 'The Best Of Me'. Once again produced by Pedro Ferreira, it was a righteous sonic assault that caused even the most jaded critics to cower in respect and awe.

In *NME,* Paul Moody bucked the paper's recent editorial trend: 'The cheesiest, filthiest guitar riff since Urge Overkill's "Sister Havana" starts up on endless, brainless repeat. A scab-infested bass belches into life with the grace and poetry of Nick Oliveri throwing up on the hard shoulder just outside Sheffield. *Get Your Hands Off My Woman* sees The Darkness attain new heights of schlock-rock genius.'

Kerrang! maintained its strong support by installing the song as Single of the Week. Although each of the three pressings of the *I Believe In A Thing Called Love* EP had dented the lower reaches of the UK top 200, the news that the new single had entered the chart at #43 came as an unexpected surprise.

'How many unsigned bands have made it into the top 40 with a song that features the word "motherfucker" eight times?', exclaimed Justin. Whilst his hypersonic profanities may have startled both the easily-offended and their dogs in equal measure, the clean version got plenty of airplay. Modestly soldiering through, Justin confessed to feeling ambivalent about

Justin makes a dive for the camera during a July 2003 photo shoot.

The Darkness play up to the camera during the Leeds festival, August 2003.

his sudden elevation to the ranks of the radio star: 'I can live with hearing the single on the radio but it's a bit hard listening to your own voice. Freaks you out a bit.'

The support tour reached its conclusion at the Brixton Academy on 27 February. In a review for *Bang* magazine (which concentrated on The Darkness rather than the night's headliners), Suzy West emphatically returned Justin's trademark 'thumbs up': 'The Darkness put on a show and play rock stars, but the songs are completely prog-free and balls out . . . they're so masculine you could get impregnated standing too near the front.'

Such tongue-in-cheek exultation was analysed by rock writer Alexis Petridis in the previous day's *Guardian*. In an insightful article, Petridis nailed the tendency of the self-consciously hip to mitigate their enjoyment of an uncool genre, by perceiving it as 'ironic': 'It's hard to suppress a rush of excitement when confronted with the synthetic blast of Van Halen's "Jump" or the opening riff of "Smoke On The Water". If you smirk, it covers up the fact that you're actually enjoying yourself in the most straightforward way imaginable.'

But there were still enough punters ready to discard the knotty issue of irony and buy the single, which remained in the top 75 for a second week. Flush with chart success, but still scraping by on £10 a day, the band eagerly seized the opportunity for some free *vol-au-vents* by appearing at the *Jackass: The Movie* launch party. *Jackass* main man, and noted torturer of sleeping fathers, Bam Margera was understandably impressed: 'There's no-one else out there with the balls and fearlessness to do what they do. I think they're going to blow America apart.'

Although not yet on the scale Bam predicted, The Darkness returned to the USA in early March. The group had been invited back by the South by Southwest festival, to play their British stage. Whilst the previous year's US performance had coincided with the emotional shit hitting the fan, Dan was looking forward to playing to an American audience again. 'When we were having a hard time getting taken seriously in Britain,' he reflected, 'we did shows at South by Southwest and in LA and were well received. People don't give a shit there.'

Their triumphant, sold-out gig at the Ritz, Austin saw them described by US magazine *Blender* as 'brilliant . . . the best band there.' Ed Graham was delighted by the intense interest in the band – and by all the food on offer: 'The South by Southwest show went really well. There was loads of industry there, British and American; all the music companies were buying us steak in the best places. They took us to one of the most expensive restaurants in town and would buy us steak and lobster that cost $60 a plate. It was like a double-decker.'

However, in a review that hardened their attitude toward the band from one of mild scepticism to something approaching hatred, *NME* insisted, 'The Darkness, like Ali G, came to America and America saw through the bullshit.'

Understandably, Ed was less than delighted. 'If someone doesn't like you, they don't like you but just to write lies all the time just to slate you, it's really offensive.' Such spite had even managed to upset Harry Hawkins. 'My Dad said, 'cos he's a builder, if you do that sort of thing in the building trade and you see the person who's done that, basically lying about your work, he sees that as somebody trying to affect our career,' recalled Justin. 'So he said, "When you know that character is in the pub tell me and I'll fucking take his head off!" I was like, "Nice one Dad. Last time I heard you swear was when I was eleven and that was *bleeding*." But he obviously feels very strongly about it because it's his boys' careers.'

Frankie wore the stoic visage that has melted the heart of many a good woman, and struck fear into many a bad man. 'Is this a face of concern? We wouldn't have done this if we were concerned about how people responded to it. It's great fun for us.'

Pleased that his expectations of the Stateside crowd had been validated, Dan dismissed any talk of irony. 'Rock isn't a joke in America. Just like no-one went to see Def Leppard for ironic reasons; that crowd were there because they genuinely loved rock. That's why we felt at home.'

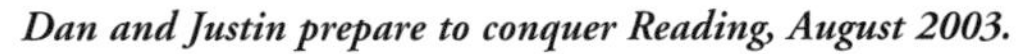

Dan and Justin prepare to conquer Reading, August 2003.

The HAMMER
GOLDEN GODS
2003
EA SPORTS
BIG

The flying visit to the US was an encouraging prelude to the band's first British headline tour. The nine-date trek was perfectly timed. The band were receiving regular attention from the music press, 'Get Your Hands Off My Woman' was continuing to pick up airplay, with the video in heavy rotation on MTV2, and two Darkness tracks had been included on free CDs with *Bang* magazine ('The Best Of Me') and *Metal Hammer* ('Stuck In A Rut').

It all served to heighten awareness of the group, as did the recording of a session for Colin Murray's Radio One programme. 'We've had hundreds of e-mails about it,' revealed a delighted Murray, 'there are so many other bands coming from the same place they are, but without the humour.'

All the touring, rehearsal and recording had also paid off. The Darkness's grand stadium sound was by now sharply defined. 'We are the nation's leading purveyors of stadium rock,' trumpeted Justin, 'This might be the last chance to see us before we actually are playing stadiums – and it will cost you four times as much then. So it's now or never. You'll also be entertained in the best possible fucking rocking way there is.'

We're an ambitious band and we want to be playing really big venues and we want to able to connect and you have to be able do that visually as well as sonically. **Justin Hawkins**

With the band's sound nailed down tighter than Justin's love pouch, plans were made to enhance the visual spectacle. 'I'm having "extra staging",' declared a delighted Justin. 'Ed will have his drum riser and above him there's going to be this curved arc that will enable me to climb up and over his. I don't know how confirmed that is though, it's just an idea right now. It demands venues with high ceilings though, or I'll just have to crawl around!'

Extra assistance was recruited to ensure Justin's mid-set costume change didn't require the opening bars of 'Stuck In A Rut' to be played more than half a dozen times. 'I am constantly looking to improve the spectacle of our shows,' enthused Justin, 'and mostly my moves are the result of on-stage improvisation – I have a tailor, Christian Hutter, who creates my on-stage look using his skill and imagination.'

With ticket sales for the tour matching the level of Justin's hyperbole, the band's scheduled London Mean Fiddler show was upgraded to the nearby Astoria. In keeping with The

Justin succumbs to festival madness at Reading, August 2003.

Frankie, Ed, Justin and Dan at the 'Metal Hammer Golden Gods Awards', July 2003.

Darkness's rising profile, press coverage of the gigs was comprehensive. Although only awarding the band a two-star rating, *Guardian* reviewer Dave Simpson nevertheless admitted they were 'very metal and often very funny'. Reporting on the group's Brighton show, *The Independent*'s Fiona Sturges was pleasantly bemused: 'The Darkness: idiots or savants? Don't ask me, but they're a cracking night out.'

Frankie seemed to understand the media's reservations: 'Sometimes the image actually works against us rather than for us. More often than not it makes press concentrate on image and not appreciate the songs.'

'If the press aren't taking it seriously then screw them,' declared Justin. 'At the end of the day if they don't believe in it we don't need them. We're putting out our own single and album. We've never been prepared to play the game. Image is important.'

As the tour progressed, Frankie was delighted by the diversity of the crowds. 'We're crossing barriers. We're surprising ourselves, seeing the kind of people we're crossing over to – IT and office workers, indie crowds and hard-rockers. When we supported Def Leppard, we had these hard-rockers come over with their kids in tow. They were teenagers, who were into nu-metal, and their dads were bringing them along and saying, "This is how real rock is played." It was really encouraging.'

Camp is not a good word for us, really. I think 'macho' is more like it! What we do is not camp. **Justin Hawkins**

The band returned to London on 4 April, to record an appearance for BBC Television's *Re:Covered* programme. The show's format required the performance of a specially-selected cover version, in addition to their own material. Underlining their commitment to mischief, The Darkness plumped for a significantly livelier version of Radiohead's 'Street Spirit (Fade Out)'.

The following night's sold-out show at the Astoria would later be recalled by Justin as a career highlight. Describing the concert as 'a triumph of rock over evil', *Kerrang!* scribe Alexander Milas was in no doubt as to who the Daddy was: 'Wielding his axe like a sceptre, rock-gymnast Justin seems like a king – the crowd, his subjects. Only stopping long enough to strip off and kiss his bicep, his howling vocals dance around Dan Hawkins' wailing guitar licks and Frankie Poullain's zen basslines as Ed Graham's tooth-jangling percussion sends metallic shockwaves through the crowd.'

The gig saw Justin cavorting in a variety of exciting new outfits – to the delight of both the Astoria crowd and his parents. Despite the high-embarrassment potential of watching their offspring 'moon' his arse to over a thousand paying customers, he maintained that his folks couldn't have been prouder. 'Oh, it's a dream come true for them. They think we're like the Jackson Two or something!'

Writing in the *Daily Star*, Sean Hamilton negotiated the irony maze with a perceptiveness that has thus far eluded the *NME*: 'Their shrieking falsettos, ear-piercing guitar solos and surprisingly great songs are the perfect antidote to serious Coldplay and bland pop. Their tanked-up fans treat every gig as the mother of all nights out – as do the band.'

With penetration of the tabloids complete, The Darkness had ascended another rung on their climb to the rock summit. 'I don't think it has taken that long really for people to catch

The band assemble at HMV Records, Oxford Street, on the day of 'Permission To Land's' release, July 2003.

on,' observed Justin 'A band's not a proper band till they've played 200 gigs, so we're only just getting there.'

As the band followed the tour with minor adjustments to their already-completed debut album, the long awaited major-label bidding war began to materialise. Although the initial plan was to release the album on Must Destroy, the possibility of signing to a big label caused some hesitancy. 'There were loads of other labels interested in the band and our deal was taking ages and the longer it was taking it was becoming increasingly apparent that they were going to get signed to a major,' revealed Ian Johnsen. 'But we all wanted to work together because we had become friends while the deal with the majors was getting sorted.'

Although Sony and East West were emerging as front-runners for the band's signature, the lack of a closed deal was symptomatic of a climate of caution in the music business. 'Lots of record label people would come to the gigs time and time again and say they loved it, but said they would never be able to sign them,' revealed Sue Whitehouse. Johnsen concurred. 'Everyone else had seen them and turned them down,' he said. 'They are no different now to how they were then.'

'It was mad,' recalled Dan, 'we were too busy to have even part-time jobs and though we

The band arrive for the Mercury Music Prize awards, September 2003.

were selling out the Astoria we still didn't have any money. We had proved we had a fan base and were getting as much press as some signed bands but they still didn't want to know. Then a month later we were suddenly in the middle of a bidding war.'

Ultimately, East West took the plunge and signed The Darkness on 12 May 2003. Managing director Korda Marshall was delighted with his latest acquisition, offering a highly individual explanation of the group's appeal: 'Like all great talent they are unique and individual and can't be put into a box. They are so unfashionable they are now fashionable, which in turn has made them unfashionable with the people that thought being uncool is fashionable. It's quite a bizarre position.'

Customarily upbeat, Justin saw advantages in the protracted wait for a deal. 'In a way we've A&R'd ourselves because we haven't had an external force come in and pay for things and tell us to do this, that and the other. All the bits of input we've had we've completely ignored – for example someone says tone it down so we bring out more catsuits and make it more high key – and we've concentrated on songwriting.'

Dan identified 'bloody-mindedness' as the motivating factor behind the band: 'We've become this unit doing what we want. Everyone else can either beat us or join us and it doesn't look like they've got much option at the moment.'

Their deal with East West also provided the foursome with an opportunity to dress up as eighteenth-century noblemen for the signing ceremony. 'Because they could,' ran the explanation in their official statement.

For The Darkness, the retention of their independent promotional and distribution team was an important facet of the deal with East West. 'We were fortunate because East West reimbursed us for all the money we spent on putting out their first singles and Alan and I are still A&R consultants and so are still kept in the loop,' Ian Johnsen explained.

'They were the company that agreed to take on the team that were working for us up to the point of us getting a record deal,' confirmed Justin of East West, 'we sold out without selling out.'

As part of this arrangement, the band's third single, 'Growing On Me', was issued on the Must Destroy label. While East West A&R chief Max Lousada negotiated a worldwide distribution deal with Atlantic, the band set to work on a video to promote the disc. Directed by Alex Smith (who previously worked with the Beatings and Six By Seven), the video referenced all the classic rock clichés associated with Van Halen, Queen and Whitesnake (whom the band supported in Ipswich on 10 May).

'We play space lords of the manor in this video,' announced Justin. 'Obviously, the pterodactyl rape scene won't feature heavily on *CD:UK*, but it works. Nudity is a recurring theme because the kids love it. It felt comfortable getting my kit off because they promised to blank out my crown jewels and it's all in the name of tasteful art.'

Some careful pixellation spared Justin's clutter further exposure, and the video quickly became an MTV staple. With a forthcoming album and single to promote, The Darkness returned to live action. A pair of warm-up dates in Middlesbrough and Guildford acted as preparation for an epic summer of touring and festival appearances. 'We'll do as many as we can,' proclaimed Dan, 'we're totally a festivals band. Festivals, weddings, parties, that's our forte.'

It's a whole different kettle of fish doing festivals. All the processes and the meticulous sound quality things you've got when you're on tour just get thrown out the window. **Dan Hawkins**

The Darkness made their festival debut at the spiritual home of outdoor metal, Donington Park in Leicestershire. The Download festival was organised to fill the gap in the summer schedule usually occupied by the Ozzfest. On a line-up headlined by Iron Maiden, Metallica and Marilyn Manson, The Darkness popped their Donington cherry with a half-hour set on the main stage during the second day.

Sadly, Justin was unable to fulfil his ambition to be fired from a cannon during the show: 'Once they've rebuilt Wembley and renamed it The Darkness Stadium, we'll play there and I'll be fired onstage as a human cannonball, I'll hit the wall, slide down and start the first track.'

Still, he was delighted to survive his rite of passage at Donington. 'There were a few people down the front who were determined to take the piss out of us, making "wanker" signs at me and calling me a faggot and stuff. But they were just waiting for some wank-turd wrestling-rock band like Disturbed to come on. A few guys out of 50,000 is pretty good. I thought we'd get bottled off after five minutes.'

A fortnight later the band appeared at the Isle of Wight festival, supporting flaccid Canadian pop-rocker Bryan Adams. The following day, 16 June, saw the release of the *Growing On Me* EP. Backed by live opener 'Bareback' and the anthemic Queen pastiche 'How Dare You Call This Love?', the single burst into the UK chart at number eleven before drifting out of the top 30 three weeks later.

The band pose with the silverware at The Mercury Music prize show. The title was later awarded to rapper Dizzee Rascal, September 2003.

'It's like having two number ones, and it's one louder than ten,' declared Dan with just a hint of *Spinal Tap*. 'We haven't even started releasing our really good songs yet.' Reviewing the single for the *Dotmusic.com* site, Chris Heath enthused, '"Growing On Me" is just one of many classics in waiting with Justin Hawkins' falsetto in full swing and a guitar solo that will make grown man weep. Resist them at your peril, just watch them grow and grow.'

With advance orders for the album streaming in, the band enjoyed the opportunity of stretching out on two of the UK's largest stages with a pair of shows supporting rock heavy-weights Deep Purple and Lynyrd Skynrd at Birmingham NEC and Wembley Arena. Although pleased to be back on the road, Justin seemed more delighted to have put the days of the Volkswagen camper behind him: 'The tour bus is the best thing on earth! It's a mobile pub 'til seven o'clock in the morning every night of the week. You can get completely wrecked and then shut yourself up in a bunk and wake up at four pm the next day in a different town. We're a band that had to be on tour – we didn't get into rock 'n' roll to live in the real world.'

10.15 on a Friday morning is not the optimum time of day for balls-out rock. Regardless of the early start, The Darkness were determined to open the Glastonbury festival with a jack-hammer wake-up call. Keen to 'take what could be a shitty slot and make it something special,' Justin adopted a resolutely positive attitude – 'It's the prime slot actually 'cause it's the ceremonial opening of the festival.'

'It's a test for our fans. We want to see how much they love us,' added Frankie. The band's short set opened with Justin asking the bleary-eyed crowd if they believed in rock before breakfast. Although unaccustomed to such rock grandiosity so early in the day, the crowd responded warmly to The Darkness's infectious sense of fun.

'We had a brilliant turn out and it went well,' affirmed Ed. Managing to squeeze in a short

The Artist at the Mercury Music Prize bash, September 2003.

Panasonic
2003
Mercury
ARTIST

JACK DANIEL'S
No 7

review of the band's set between lengthy adorations of Radiohead and glossy posters of REM, *NME* doled out some begrudging praise: 'for a group who've based their entire aesthetic on Queen's "Bohemian Rhapsody" video, The Darkness are absurdly entertaining,' wrote Piers Martin.

But the head of steam built up by the band over the past year made the derision seem out-of-touch. As Justin discovered, the music paper seemed to be attempting a U-turn. 'We opened the festival, did a really good show, and the [*NME*] editor came up to me and tapped me on the shoulder. He goes, "You're going to hate me when I tell you who I am." And he told me and I said, "Fuck off then, just fuck off," and I kept saying, "Fuck off," to him because I was really angry. Then he got down on one knee and said, "I'm really sorry. We backed the wrong horse, we should have backed you." And that's what we find offensive. It's not his job to second-guess what's going to be big and popular, it's his job to write about what's happening in music. They saw us as a force that needed to be extinguished and that's what they tried, unsuccessfully, to do.'

Undaunted by the capriciousness of the music press, Justin's thoughts moved on to the idea of returning to headline the festival: 'next year we'll arrive by horse-and-cart wearing Hessian sacks. Because we're a basic Glastonbury band – a hippy rock band. Peace!'

'Next year it's going to be a big thing, opening Glastonbury, and that's because of us,' added Frankie.

We've always behaved like stadium rockers. Even at the beginning when we were playing in pubs. This is our manor. **Justin Hawkins**

As the release date of The Darkness's debut album, *Permission To Land*, approached, anticipation levels rose. Justin was quick to fan the flames of expectation. 'Right now British music is the laughing stock of the world because it's such fucking dreary bullshit. It's such a cliché to say, "We were so bored of the industry around us that we started our own band!", but it's no coincidence that all our influences are from a long time ago. And, in all seriousness, I think our album will change a lot of people's lives.'

The measure of the group's impact was borne out by a chance encounter in Belsize Park with a notorious mono-browed Mancunian misery-guts. 'A blacked-out van stopped next to us and Liam Gallagher jumped out,' recounted Justin. 'He walked straight up to us and goes, "Top band, man, top baaand, top baaand." And I went, "Ooohh, thank you." [Then] he just got back into his van and drove off. It freaked me out, actually, because that had been the most famous person I had ever met up to that point.'

Frankie offered a more impressionistic version of the meeting: 'It was a nice moment, a moment – how would I describe it? – like when Proust dips his teacake in his hot beverage.' Pressed to clarify, the bassist explained, 'in his *Remembrance of Things Past* he dipped his teacake in his hot beverage and that reminded him of his childhood. Liam Gallagher was the tea cake.'

The younger Gallagher was swiftly ousted from the top of Justin's personal fame parade, when the band undertook two dates supporting panto-rock legend Alice Cooper – the second alongside sixties psych-garage pioneer Arthur Love and old mates the Wildhearts at the annual Guildford GuilFest. An appearance on *Later with Jools Holland* saw a catsuited Justin dancing atop the host's treasured piano, as a befuddled Holland struggled manfully to con-

Dan looking mighty fine in some new duds, September 2003.

tain his astonishment. The honky-tonk hunchback later congratulated the band for the best rock performance ever seen on the show.

Justin's former technical college lecturer, Charlie Griffiths caught the broadcast: 'I didn't even recognise Justin. I saw . . . this amazing singer who jumped on to the top of a grand piano, then leapt to the ground as the song ended. I thought they were brilliant. Then three days later, in college, someone said to me did you see Justin? I couldn't believe it.'

Before jetting off for their continental debut, an appearance at the With Full Force Festival in Leipzig, Germany, the band found time to appear on the Saturday morning TV chart showcase *CD:UK*. A typically ebullient rendition of 'Growing On Me' left a lasting impression on presenter Cat Deeley: 'Now there is a band who don't know the meaning of the words "less is more"!'

Permission To Land was released under the Must Destroy/Atlantic subsidiary on 7 July 2003. Alternate titles suggested by Justin had included *Death In Both Ears, Women Who Exaggerate, All Puns Blazing* and *Thank You, This Will Suffice For Me, Now If You Please Some Sex For My Friends.*

Recorded at Chapel Studios in Lincolnshire, the album – like the three earlier singles – was produced by Pedro Ferreira. 'We did it in two weeks working really hard on it, rehearsing it like crazy for twelve hours a day,' recalls Dan. 'We averaged about two hours sleep a night when recording because we did it all live . . . It was hard work.'

How many unsigned bands have made it into the top forty with a song that features the word 'motherfucker' eight times? Justin Hawkins

Creating an authentic reproduction of their gargantuan live sound was particularly important to Dan. 'I can't remember the last time I heard something new that hasn't been computerised and fiddled about with – but that's not the way we make records. Listen to Led Zep, listen to Queen, and you can hear people trying to play their instruments, and sometimes failing. If everything's perfect then you're in trouble, in my book, and I think the kids appreciate that you can feel the band actually playing.'

'It's all about the cake and the icing,' ejaculated Justin. 'The cake takes the time: You're whipping up the eggs, the sugar; that's us spending time working up the songs and the structure . . . There's just no way that we'd be doing this for a joke because it's taken up the best years of our lives.'

DJ Colin Murray agreed: 'The album isn't at all about being novelty. It might have "Get Your Hands Off My Woman, Motherfucker" on there but it's also got a couple of major rock anthems.'

The live favourite 'Black Shuck' kicks off the ten tracks on the disc, promptly followed by each of the band's earlier A-sides ('Get Your Hands Off My Woman', 'Growing On Me' and 'I Believe In A Thing Called Love'). The remainder of the album is divided between sweeping power ballads ('Love Is Only A Feeling', 'Love On The Rocks With No Ice' and 'Holding My Own'), and high-octane stompers ('Givin' Up', 'Stuck In A Rut' and 'Friday Night').

In an Xfm interview, the brothers Hawkins waxed surreal regarding the album's scope. 'It's a total rock feast,' declared Dan. 'It covers a lot of angles that no one's touched for years. It's got everything. It's like harvest festival . . .'

'Where everyone's brought their unwanted food to the table and made a delicious meal for

Justin channels the spirit of Jimi Hendrix at the Isle of Wight Festival, May 2003

Dan, Justin and Frankie on stage at New York's Irving Plaza, November 2003.

the starving,' added Justin. 'And it's all going to go off very soon. It ranges from the stripped-down hard-rocking rock to the more luxurious success-related end of it and that's just the production. There's a common thread and that's the songwriting.'

'There's a guitar solo on every song,' chimed in Frankie.

The group spent release day promoting *Permission To Land* with a live appearance on the Xfm *Breakfast Session* and an in-store gig at HMV Oxford Street. A 1,500-strong crowd turned out to see the band perform a seven-song set, causing fans to spill out onto the street.

The critics were equally enthusiastic. In *The Telegraph*, Ian Douglas foresaw a bright future for the group: 'The Darkness will be huge. They will be enormous rock stars, selling out Wembley and spending years on tour trying to break America. They will probably succeed.'

Visions of 'Planet Darkness' were glimpsed in Rob Kemp's *Rolling Stone* review: '*Permission*

To Land is the first retro-metal album that's worth more than a momentary chuckle. Eighties hard rock is alive and well in the hands of the Darkness.'

'When you listen to the record,' observed Justin, helpfully, 'it gives off the same sort of feeling as sharing a tent in the Amazon with Brian Eno.'

The midweek chart positions showed *Permission To Land* touching down at number two, kept from the top spot by Beyonce's *Dangerously In Love.* Within two weeks it had passed the 100,000-sales mark, leaving Justin in valedictory mood. 'We feel vindicated, lubricated, but ultimately appreciated. It feels like we're feasting at the captain's table from a banquet where every flower reveals itself.'

Warming to his topic, the front man described *Permission To Land* as 'less of a request to moor the good ship Darkness, rather a demand to shift the rest of the shit cluttering up rock's runway.' Coming down to earth slightly, he conceded, 'As a debut album it is up there with the best debut albums ever because it sounds huge, and the songs are brilliant. I'm proud of all of it. There is nothing concept about it, nothing funny, just a proper rocking album.'

Justin on stage at New York's Irving Plaza, November 2003.

5

Men That Do Rock, Baby

There's nothing else like us around. And that's really sad. What's happened to this sweet nation if we haven't got two decent rock bands? There's no-one anywhere near us, and that's what people find amusing about it. **Justin Hawkins**

Permission To Land catapulted The Darkness into the mainstream of British pop culture. With the announcement of a trio of dates supporting ubiquitous family favourite Robbie Williams at Knebworth, their birthright of playing before six-figure crowds was about to be realised. The tabloid press also discovered the band, and the relentless heat of summer 2003 was matched by the swirling clouds of hyperbole that enveloped them.

Writing in classic *Sun*-speak, Victoria Newton proclaimed, 'Take a good look at this bunch of Spandex-clad, pelvic-thrusting nutters – they may well be the saviours of British music.' Whilst many neophyte celebrities struggle to cope with the pressures of media interest, Justin's acquired savvy and 4-D personality ensured he knew *precisely* how to manipulate the fame game, and titillate *The Sun*'s readership: 'We're going to be Number Two and Beyonce's going to be Number One. Underneath Beyonce's not a bad place to be, if you know what I mean.'

Declaring himself delighted with all the attention, he admitted, 'At the moment the

Justin unveils another Lucy Manning designed catsuit for the 2003 MTV Europe Music Awards, November 2003.

Frankie and Justin with DJ Sara Cox, at Radio 1's 'One Big Weekend' event, September 2003.

tabloid coverage is great. When they are being nice to you, they are really nice. I get *The Sun* phoning me up saying, "There's been no one to write about except Liam Gallagher for ten years and then you came along." They even apologised for sending someone round to my mum's for baby photos. But we know it can't last and we are ready for people to turn on us; that's fair enough. Hopefully by then we will have found our audience and a whole load more people will know what we do.'

Similarly, both Hawkins brothers were keen to break into primetime and daytime TV. 'I'll do anything that Jon Bon Jovi has been on – guest appearances on *Ally McBeal*, that sort of thing,' announced Justin. 'Having said that, Richard and Judy and Des and Mel are definitely on the agenda.'

'We want to hunt for rock memorabilia with David Dickinson,' said Dan. 'He's a sizeable man. Surprisingly tall in the flesh.' Agog at the whole learning experience, Frankie observed, 'We've had the chance to see ourselves on telly recently and that's great for us. We can take it further and that's what we've done the last three years, not just willy-nilly.'

We've got high-profile female fans – Zoe Ball and Jo Whiley, who tend to point out the muscular nature of my abdomen, which can only be encouraged. **Justin Hawkins**

For the time being however, Justin was content just to enjoy being noticed. 'People used to look at me funny because I'm a bit of a bell-end but now it's because they've seen me on the telly.'

Before Justin introducing Freddie Mercury imitators on *Stars In Their Eyes* became a lysergic reality, however, the band had a number of prior engagements to fulfil. First up was an appearance on the main stage of Scotland's T In The Park festival. It represented something of a homecoming for Frankie, who was brought up in nearby Milnathort, and before the gig he was delighted to receive support from an unlikely source. 'We got a lovely e-mail from Fran Healy from Travis the

Jo Whiley meets the star at the Radio 1 'One Big Weekend' festival. (09/03)

other day. He was saying that his band struggled in a similar way to us for years without any recognition. So we'd love to hook up with him sometime.'

Suitably encouraged, The Darkness put in a tremendous set that saw a sea of raised thumbs out on the horizon. Promoter Dave McGeachan saw the gig as a turning point for the band. 'It went bonkers after T In The Park, that changed a lot of people's cynical ideas about them,' he observed of their progress north of the border. 'They only played Tut's [King Tut's Wah Wah Hut – one of Glasgow's small-sized venues] six months ago, but they could easily play to 20,000 people now – that's two SECCs [Glasgow's largest concert hall]. If they were to announce an SECC gig right now, it would sell out in a matter of hours.'

Frankie with his mum (kneeling), and other family members at the 'T In The Park Festival', July 2003.

Frankie was overjoyed with the turn-out. 'People said we had a bigger crowd than REM the night before. The crowd went right back to the hotdog stands right at the back.' Andrew Perry's *Telegraph* review identified the group as the festival's star turn: 'The sight of Darkness singer Justin Hawkins, clad in a tiger-print leotard, teaching the sun dazed throng to sing in falsetto, was perhaps the defining moment of a hugely entertaining weekend.'

The 35,000 that turned out for T In The Park may have seemed a sizeable crowd, but, compared with the estimated 325,000 punters who showed up for Robbie Williams' Knebworth concerts, it was just a short queue for the toilet. Given that The Darkness were to perform on the sort of gargantuan stage they'd always dreamed of, Justin was keen to ensure that everything went off (and on) smoothly. 'The costumes are having to be chiselled on rather than sewn,' he elaborated. 'They'll be really spectacular. Because I've got to change quickly I'll be going commando. It's a case of greasing round the scrotum with Swarfega and shaving my buttocks so nothing catches on the fabric.'

Although the unflappable Frankie saw the shows as simply 'another festival', Ed confessed to some nerves: 'We didn't even have time to have a rehearsal before Knebworth. It was like,

"Fucking hell, we're playing to, like, 375,000 people," and we hadn't even had a rehearsal.'

Regardless of being scheduled to go on first, ahead of wimp-rockers Ash and the summer's favourite missile target, Kelly Osbourne, Justin remained assured of following manfully in the footsteps of Led Zeppelin and Queen: 'A band of our ilk is genetically determined to achieve the honour of performing at Knobwerth [sic]. It's in our DNA. We've waited years for this opportunity and we're truly grateful and honoured to have been invited. Treading those hallowed boards will have as much emotional impact for me as stepping out on to the pitch at St James' Park has for a Geordie soccer enthusiast.'

Describing the make-up of the all-ages crowd, *NME* adopted a typically haughty tone: 'There are women in their early-thirties wearing T-shirts saying, "Robbie's Girl", tattooed England supporters, families and people waving St George's flags and various inflatable objects including a penis and a Spider-Man. Naff Britain in a microcosm.'

Such anti-proletarian posturing was irrelevant as far as The Darkness were concerned – they knew that the Robbie crowd *are* the mainstream. For a band that cares infinitely more about providing an audience with entertainment than they do about any kind of arbitrary credibility, it was *exactly* the type of crowd they should be playing to. 'Rock and roll isn't about being cool – it's about breaking rules,' insisted Frankie. 'And the biggest rule at the moment is that you have to be cool. Being cool is just being boring, being average.'

Robbie was like John Travolta in Grease when he's with all his mates. **Frankie Poullain**

In contrast to snobbish music press reviews, *Sun* correspondent Victoria Newton gave a down to earth report, 'At precisely 2.56pm Knebworth was starting to fill up – and the assembled crowd got a wake-up call like no other. Bare-chested Justin Hawkins from The Darkness screamed to the fans: "Show me your thumbs" and the front 278 rows or so duly obliged. Then one of Britain's most refreshing rock bands proceeded to shake the Hertfordshire estate to its foundations with one of the most energetic sets I have ever seen.'

The initially stunned crowd reacted with a growing warmth, as the messianic Justin rapidly converted all before him. His unauthorised caper along Robbie's personal section of the stage delighted onlookers, and the group departed to a tumultuous reception. Overjoyed by the audience response, and unabashed by showing them his bum during the costume change, Justin sought out Robbie Williams: 'I went to say thanks because it was a great opportunity for us and I think we delivered. He let me through his entourage of security and said to me: "I love all your stuff, Moby." . . . . but he didn't bother to watch us.'

Unable to summon up any sense of fun, *NME* opted to get personal on Justin's perfectly-proportioned ass. 'Seeing Justin's craggy, allegedly 27-year-old face on the enormous screens calls to mind one of the late Bob Hope's old jokes: "She says she's approaching 40, although I don't know from which direction."'

Contrasting the support of *Kerrang!* with *NME*'s constant sniping, Justin rationalised, '*Kerrang!* built us up and they're perfectly within their rights to knock us down now. They've given us everything they can give us and been really supportive whereas the *NME* have just knocked us down. In a way their love is more intense. It's more about a humanistic passion for us as people rather than the music. They know that we're newsworthy really but their idea is that if they can't have us then no one can have us. They'd rather destroy us than let someone else . . . bed us.'

"They think we're the Jackson Two" – The Brothers Hawkins.

Dan and Justin at the Kerrang! Awards, August 2003.

In a major *volte-face*, the 2 August edition of *NME* (or 'New Musical Spandexpress', as the paper's subheading proclaimed) featured a rampant Justin on the cover, in addition to a four-page feature on the band. Whilst a quarter of the item was given over to dressing up reporter Marc Hayward *a la* Justin, it was clear that the ailing music paper could no longer afford to traduce the nation's foremost rock group. About to undergo a major restructuring after plummeting sales, editorial policy could no longer stand in the way of shifting a few extra units by sticking Justin's splendid visage on the cover.

It cut little ice with Justin himself. 'You wouldn't think the *NME* would sell their readers short by putting a band on the cover without an interview. We're boycotting them. They have no chance with any of us ever co-operating with them. I don't care if we're cutting off our noses to spite our faces, I'd rather not have a face at all. They're a bunch of inadequate journalists that know nothing. This is war.'

As he put his tin hat on, the news came in that they'd been nominated for three *Kerrang!* awards as well as the coveted Mercury Music Prize. With *Permission To Land* already having achieved gold disc status, The Darkness picked up further commemorative bric-a-brac at the annual *Kerrang!* awards at London's Royal Lancaster Hotel, on 21 August. Scooping both the Best Album and Best Live Act categories, they crowned a triumphant evening with a typically energetic rendition of 'I Believe In A Thing Called Love'.

Despite being beaten (incredibly) to the Best British Newcomer gong by Funeral For A Friend, Justin seemed happy enough. 'We'd just missed out on an award so it was two out of three for us. I was just thinking, "Two out of three ain't bad." I was thinking – we're a Meatloaf song!'

Looking for all the world like Eli Wallach in *The Good, the Bad and the Ugly* gone metal, Frankie offered a spiritual perspective to *Kerrang!* readers: 'Believe in the dream. Hold the dream. Nurture the dream. Live the dream. And one day the dream will come true.'

Whatever post-dream hangovers the band may have been nursing were not in evidence when they took the main stage at Reading the next day. As the most rock-orientated of the UK's summer festivals, the twin Reading and Leeds events provided the opportunity to play to a crowd that required little winning over.

With his voice beginning to feel the strain of the band's relentless schedule, Justin's vocal warm ups became increasingly vital, October 2003.

'I'm looking forward to Reading because I used to go there,' announced Justin. 'I went there five years on the trot. Me and Ed used to run a thing we called the "Fun Centre", which was like a circle of canvas tents and people would just drop in. It was built around the foundation of very heavy drinking and white cider. And there were power-drinking competitions wearing a special cape whilst standing in the most macho way you can.'

The Darkness's rapid increase in popularity, combined with rapper Jay-Z's late withdrawal, saw the band elevated from the Radio One Tent to the Main Stage. They followed a bizarre set from sulky nu-metallers Staind, which only the band and their crew could actually hear. Amidst the Quo-like strains of 'Bareback', the sudden arrival of The Darkness into the glorious early evening sunlight could not have presented a greater contrast. As with T In The Park, the band made the festival their own.

There's nothing rebellious about standing in a field full of Marilyn Manson fans with your finger in the air, because everyone else is doing it. Let's do something different. **Justin Hawkins**

Justin strikes a pose at Knebworth, August 2003.

Throughout the weekend, whole tent-fulls of burly rockers struggled manfully to match Justin's sonic warble each time a Darkness track played between sets. Even *NME*'s Steve Sutherland was impressed: 'There's only one band on the festival's collective lips this Friday and that's The Darkness. They got more T-shirts out front, more thumbs in the air, more blokes singing falsetto than any band since . . . well, probably Queen at Knebworth.'

As the first journalist to recognise the band's potential, Simon Price allowed himself a degree of self-satisfaction: 'In 2003, suddenly and gratifyingly, the world has finally woken up to The Darkness. Throughout a summer in which they have tirelessly played every festival on the calendar and supported the likes of Def Leppard, Deep Purple, Meat Loaf, Metallica, Robbie and, shortly, the Rolling Stones, the shameless efferves-

The band in a relaxed mode at a photoshoot, August 2003.

cence of the band's showmanship has picked up thousands of new fans, causing an irresistible snowball effect. After years of mass-marketed miserablism and fake angst, The Darkness aren't simply the band who have put a smile back on the face of music – they might just be the band who save rock 'n' roll.' Naturally, Justin agreed. 'We'll be headlining arenas by next year. They can't wait, it's going to be fucking Beatlemania.'

Amidst this welter of activity, the band prepared for a brief tour of Germany. The largest of the German dates was a gig supporting the Rolling Stones at Hanover's cavernous Open Air Arena. Resisting the temptation to contrast his excellent Mick Jagger impersonation with the original article, Justin was obviously excited at meeting the legendary grandfathers of rock. 'Mick just popped his head round the corner and said, "Hello, all right?" Then Keith came in, eyes wobbling, living it, really living the dream, you know, still doing it.'

The admiration was reciprocated, with Sir Mick admiring Justin's vinyl loons. 'Mick says he really likes them. But I don't think he could really be bothered with the 30 minutes it takes to get into them and then you have to allow that again every time you need the toilet,' revealed the frontman.

With the release date of the band's fourth single (a reissue of 'I Believe In A Thing Called Love') set for 22 September, The Darkness returned to England to begin work on a new video. Once again directed by Alex Smith, the promo represented a natural progression for the band – with the UK conquered and the US in their sights, it was only fitting that the video took the band into outer space.

Smith depicted the band as rock's Jedi Knights, destroying cosmic evil with the power of

a few well-executed solos. 'When we did "Growing On Me" we just had Alex with his little camera and the whole budget was minuscule, he basically just worked his ass off and I don't think he paid himself anything to make it happen,' Justin explained. 'This time he managed to assemble a whole team of people; cameramen, runners, health and safety officers, producers and set builders. It was a really amazing experience 'cos there were like 20 or 30 people working on the set with us, and just pandering to our every request. So we got the chance to act like real prima donnas – fabulous experience. That's why we're in this game; for the opportunity to have massive tantrums and behave like complete idiots.'

Following an open-air gig at the Rockingham racetrack in Northamptonshire and a brief excursion to play a small show in Den Bosch, Holland, The Darkness returned home to find *Permission To Land* touted as a favourite for the Mercury Best Album Prize. Indeed, the *NME* – accompanied by the sound of furious back-pedalling – pronounced them winners on the day before the actual event.

Before the show, Dan was sanguine about the band's prospects. 'I think in a way we've won already because so many people were chuffed to hear we were nominated. We don't stand a chance. The whole thing is a highbrow overview and we aren't highbrow. We're just a band to be enjoyed. It would be hilarious if we won and brilliant too because it would pay for the suits we're planning to wear to the ceremony. If you see us looking unhappy when we don't win it's only because we'll be sat there in £20,000 worth of Gucci suits with no-one to pay for them.'

Ridicule is nothing to be scared of. **Justin Hawkins (quoting Adam Ant)**

Ultimately, the band were beaten to the award by rapper Dizzee Rascal's *Boy In Da Corner*. 'We're glad we didn't win,' claimed Dan. 'We respect the Mercury Prize but it would not have been right for us to win it so early in our career.' Justin was less stoical, irritated by the muted response to The Darkness's performance. 'They were tepid. Tepid to warm I think. More of the tepid to cold then really, weak on many levels. It wasn't really a gig-going crowd, they were diners – they were *vol-au-vent* scoffers. They weren't fists in the air, they were knives and forks, poised above some melon and Parma ham or something, they weren't ready for us I don't think.'

Putting any disappointment behind them, The Darkness warmed up for three sold-out US/Canadian shows, plus appearances at the One Big Weekend event in Cardiff and another gig supporting the Stones at Wembley Arena. With *Permission To Land* rush-released on 16 September to coincide with shows in New York, Toronto and Los Angeles, Justin was in a positive mood: 'Rock music is kicking arse again – it's a sign of the times that the forthcoming Bon Jovi, AC/DC, Aerosmith and KISS tours are among the most anticipated music events for ages. People are beginning to cherish the old values, and thanks to Busted, nu-metal is croaking its last death rattle, even as we speak. With a bit of luck, The Darkness will be driving the next bandwagon that everybody jumps on – but don't forget, we were around before classic rock was fashionable, and we'll still be around when it goes out again.'

Despite Justin's ebullience, Ed harboured no illusions about the size of the task ahead of them. 'America is a difficult place to break as a British band. Many bands that are massive here have gone over and then not done very well over there.'

Dan, however, saw the dates as a launch-pad for greater success. 'We're going to go and say "hello" to America and then next year we're going to move in . . . . There's New York and LA, the cool parts where they're receptive to British bands. But there's also the bit in between, which is vast, and highly populated. And that's where we're at. We have no concept of being

Justin seduces the crowd into a singalong while supporting Metallica at Dublin's RDS, August 2003.

cool. If anything, we fight it. And those people will get off on it.'

'The whole thing that's held us back here has been, "Are they taking the piss?",' observed Frankie, 'but that isn't an issue there. We'll be judged on the merits of our performance.'

Justin, as ever, was confident. 'I think a lot of bands who go there aren't aware of what they are biting off but we've been there and done a couple of shows. We've got the hang of how to approach an audience and that's the first step. There are ways of knowing how to do it that are right and those that are obviously wrong.'

The Darkness's opening show at the Bowery Ballroom, New York, was bolstered by a considerable British contingent, their twelve-number set receiving a rapturous reception. *Spin* journalist Mark Spitz observed, 'Before the show, I told myself I'd study them and try to decide what the irony level was. But after two or three songs I didn't fucking care. Even if they're putting it on, I got off on them like it was pure, so it *was* pure. They're not parody, they're just very witty.'

Although pleased with the response, Justin retained his focus. 'This is what we've worked towards. And now we're here – it's a window of opportunity. And we're not in the habit of making the sort of mistakes that would lead to that window being slammed shut, never to be opened again. We feel ready, so it's just a matter of plugging in and going for it now.'

There's never any time to sit around sucking each other's cocks. **Frankie Poullain**

Similar enthusiasm greeted the band in Toronto, whilst the LA Roxy show attracted such luminaries as Jack Osbourne and Blink 182's Travis Barker. At the end of the final gig, Justin pledged to return for a longer tour the following year. Even the news that the American Wal-Mart and K-Mart chain stores were refusing to stock *Permission To Land* because of nudity in its cover design failed to temper their high spirits. 'Our album is selling well on import in America. But Wal-Mart won't stock it because of the woman's bum on the sleeve,' explained Frankie. 'We'll just re-shoot it and turn the naked women round so we can see it from the front instead.'

The Darkness returned to the UK to perform at the MTV2 Fifth Birthday Party, supporting Jane's Addiction at Brixton Academy. Whilst the band were in LA, 'I Believe In A Thing Called Love' had entered the UK chart at number two. It was a different version from that of the album, backed with two newer songs – 'Physical Sex' and 'Makin' Out'.

NME pronounced the song 'Pick of the Week', announcing, ironically enough, that it was 'time to get over your upright, irrational fears of prancing men in spandex and take this to Number One.' While it narrowly missed out on topping the chart (edged out by Black Eyed Peas' 'Where Is The Love?'), *Permission To Land* finally hit the top of the album chart a week later.

'Everything just snowballed,' an ecstatic Justin told Radio One. 'People were always aware of us and it seems like we've developed enough of a following to make people sit up and take notice. There are too many people interested in us for us to be ignored.'

Dan was also in a valedictory mood, venturing into his brother's verbal territory: 'We are an albatross. Albatross can fly across whole oceans. A solitary bird, like us, we are on our own, we are out there, we are on our own and fucking flying.'

'I think now it's happened 'cos we've really fine-tuned everything and become really focused,' reasoned Frankie calmly.

Some, however, were still unsure. Iron Maiden vocalist Bruce Dickinson confessed to a little confusion. 'I haven't seen them live. I can't make out whether they're taking the piss in a

Love me; love my axe – Justin in an amorous mood.

Justin takes care of his ablutions before a Leeds University show, October 2003.

very clever way or whether they're really serious and committed to rock. I have to go see them. It could be for real or he could be a manipulative, lying son of a bitch who's laughing at his audience for buying his album.'

He needn't have worried. 'We're proper rock, and there aren't many people who do that now,' countered Dan. 'That's why people think we're not for real. We're going to be one of those bands, like the Smiths, that if you try to copy you'd last two seconds. We're not four blokes trying to be another band.'

The band barely had time to toast the success of *Permission To Land* before they returned to the road. Following the 30 September Brixton date, the group headed to Dublin before returning to Britain to commence a sixteen-date tour culminating at the recently re-opened Hammersmith Apollo. The hectic schedule was intensified by the constant media demand for interviews and the recording of a Christmas single – 'Christmas Time (Don't Let The Bells End)' with former Alice Cooper/Aerosmith/Pink Floyd producer Bob Ezrin.

'The concept of the Christmas guitar single is one that has been overlooked for many moons,' insisted Justin. 'It's an art form in itself. If you do it right, you'll end up with something really, really special. Our single will be the gift that keeps on giving, year in, year out. It's a moving ballad about not being with your partner for most of the year and making the most of the holiday season. It's got a kiddies choir on it, it's got tubular bells – it's your basic full-on Christmas experience. And the chorus is world class, one bit goes, "Don't let the bells end, just let them ring in peace." It's gonna be lovely.'

A video for the single was also shot toward the end of September, depicting Justin cavorting on his yuletide love-rug before a roaring fire, and also featuring a Ferrari. 'The Ferrari is a staple image of any Christmas scene,' he explained. 'The video is a mix of every Christmas video you've ever seen in your life. The kids are wearing bobble hats, scarves and mittens tied together with string so they don't lose them on a cold winter's night. We thought about getting some elves. But we couldn't get any real ones, so we were offered a load of midgets who would have worn big ears.'

In similar festive vein, a seven-date 'Elf Hazard' tour would see the band completing their breakthrough year at some of the country's larger venues. Undaunted by the weight of their commitments, Dan was simply happy to be so busy. 'You spend years on the dole, watching daytime TV, dreaming of this moment. So we're getting really stuck into it and working our arses off. Maybe on the schedule there's like two weeks off for Christmas and that's it for the next two years but that suits me.'

On 18 October, minutes before The Darkness were due to play to a 2,000-strong house at the Liverpool Academy, Justin's voice finally gave out. The months of constant rehearsal,

The Darkness is like a sweet lady woman. You will never fully fathom it, and after a while you will stop trying because you love no other woman. **Justin Hawkins**

Justin is cornered by fans during a 'walkabout' at the Bowery Ballroom, New York, September 2003.

touring and recording had taken their toll on his larynx.

In an official statement on the band's website Justin explained what had happened to the disappointed Darklings: 'I would like to offer my sincerest apologies . . . it's the first time we've ever had to pull a show and nobody could be more disappointed than me. I've often felt a little hoarse of a morning, but usually my hour-long pre-show warm-up blows away the cobwebs. Yesterday was different, and I didn't realise how serious the problem was until around 8.30pm when my voice disappeared altogether. A doctor was called and the first thing he noticed was that one of my glands was swollen, and arranged for me to see Liverpool's finest ENT [Ear, Nose and Throat] consultant immediately, so I was driven to the hospital. He found that I have laryngitis and an infection in my voice box, I have swollen vocal chords and a troublesome node, which is (worryingly) causing mischief. If it were as simple as a sore throat, the ENT consultant could have administered an injection to reduce the swelling and the show would have gone ahead, but sadly that could not happen . . . I hope you can find it in your hearts to forgive me.'

The cancellation of two further shows, at Folkestone and Portsmouth, led the *Daily Star* to speculate that the Darkness front man may have throat cancer. When the tour resumed in Hammersmith, Justin quickly dismissed the speculation. 'Did anyone read the *Daily Star* today? That one little quote that caused a little bit of mischief? I haven't got cancer and I apologise for any concern it may have caused.' Returning to form, *NME* were inelegantly quick to provide angry fans with an e-mail address for their complaints, swiftly recycled into a 'Tour On The Rocks' storm-in-a-teacup news article.

The next album will be more of the same, and we'll try not to climb up our own arses until album three or four. **Justin Hawkins**

With the sold-out tour completed and the cancelled dates rescheduled, The Darkness sandwiched an appearance at the MTV Music Awards between a pair of German shows supporting Meatloaf. A spectacular performance at MTV's Edinburgh bash saw Justin make maximum use of an enormous walkway to show off his new £10,000 catsuit to full effect. Following a swift visit to Amsterdam, the band returned to the London Astoria for a special one-off concert. Sponsored by Carling as part of the Homecoming series of gigs that previously featured the likes of Primal Scream, the band performed before an audience of hardcore Darklings, most of whom had obtained their tickets via Darkness-themed competitions.

The show, which was filmed as part of a Channel 4 documentary on the group, was potentially the last opportunity for the faithful to see their heroes in a small venue. As the complimentary lager flowed, The Darkness ran through almost their entire recorded catalogue before the delirious crowd. There was little sign of permanent damage to Justin's voice, and he found time to fit in three full costume changes. The set concluded with a premiere of 'Christmas Time (Don't Let The Bells End)', which featured a sweetly bewildered children's choir and a hail of metallic snow that was still descending from the Astoria ceiling two nights later.

Addressing the band's loyal following directly, Justin enthused, 'Our fans are the best in the world, they don't need to be told that we're cool to be able to have a great time. When we started this band we had nothing – the music industry just didn't want to know, and because of our fans, the industry *now* recognises that we have the potential to succeed. We

Justin at the MTV2 5th birthday party at Brixton Academy, September 2003.

are nothing without you, sweet people of rock. Let's take over the fucking world together!'

The Darkness are now certified rock stars. An assault on the Christmas chart will be followed by shows in Japan and Australia, as well as a more extensive tour of the USA. Reflecting on a hectic three years, Justin took stock of events.

'When we kicked it off we thought it'd be the hugest thing in the world and everyone would go, "Fucking Hell! That's what a band used to sound like and that's how they should sound!" It'd be a fresh new sound for the kids that weren't old enough to have these stadium car park experiences. We always thought we'd be snapped up by a global conglomerate and pushed in every country in the whole wide world and be the biggest thing on earth 'cos no-one else, at that time, was doing it. But it didn't happen like that, we just got a really strong following. It's only like the last few months that we've really started kicking arse. We were just doing it 'cos we enjoyed it and if anyone else liked it, it was a bonus! But it wasn't a cynical approach. We had to rock. We couldn't stop rocking, now everyone else wants to rock as well!'

The band fully intend to keep on rocking for as long as possible. 'We are going to be here for a very long time,' promises Frankie, 'and we are going to surprise a lot of people in the process. The music industry needs us.' Justin agrees. 'We'll keep on going until we hate each other, same as any other band, it will reach its own conclusion.'

The group now have a dedicated following, and are recognised outside the parameters of rock 'n' roll. Justin has popped up in the celebrity magazine *Heat*, and the band's music can be heard as an accompaniment to such unlikely TV shows as *A Question of Sport.*

Fly fanzine editor Will Kinsman is one early supporter who would like to see The Darkness consummate their stadium dreams: 'I really hope they pull it off and in twenty years time are where AC/DC are now. I first saw them about two years ago and the whole thing about them being a joke was already happening, but I think people are taking them more seriously now. The album is great. It brings a smile to my face when I'm walking down the road with it on my Walkman. I am surprised that no-one took a punt on them earlier on as they could have signed them for £10,000 and made an album very cheaply.'

'We are here to annoy people,' insists Frankie. 'Just when you think we're gone, we are going to be there, up your arse. All the time. We are going to be in your pub. You go home to try to escape, you can switch on the radio, the TV and we are going to be there. We are going to hound and harass you.'

As ever, Justin gets the last word:

'What is the end? What is at the end of the universe and what's stopping it and what is behind what's stopping it? I am going to fake my death. I can confirm that. You may think I am dead, but I am not dead, no matter how spectacular or tangible my demise, it will not be real. You will see me in supermarkets buying things. In terms of religion I am a lion. I walk alone. I have my own personal heaven and I don't want to share it.'

Justin attempts a transatlantic flight — Bowery Ballroom, New York., September 2003.

Overleaf: The Darkness in the press. From the support of **Kerrang** ***to the bandwagon jumping of the*** **NME.**

The Darkness

FREE CD! SAVE £36! FREE HIM ART PRINT!
KERRANG!
www.kerrang.com
LIFE IS LOUD
SEPTEMBER 27
2003/ £1.90
GLASSJAW & THE USED
IN MURDER SHOCK!
THE DARKNESS
TAKE OVER THE WORLD
INSIDE:
48 HOURS ON THE ROAD WITH RANCID
LIMP BIZKIT'S NEW ALBUM: THE VERDICT
DEFTONES HIT THE UK
BRUCE DICKINSON: "MY KEBAB HELL!"
PLUS: 10 ROCK STARS IN DRAG
IF YOUR CD IS MISSING, SEE YOUR NEWSAGENT. THIS CD IS NOT AVAILABLE OUTSIDE THE UK. SORRY FOLKS.
NME
NEW MUSICAL
SPANDEXPRESS
MASSIV
TICKE
GIVEAWAY
BLACK REB
MOTORCYCLE CL
RAVEONETT
STARSAIL
V FESTIV
READING/LEEDS SOUVENIR SPECIAL
NME
MONSTER 84 PAGES!
AERIAL PHOTOS!
+ LOADS OF POSTERS
NME
NEW LOOK!
NEW MUSICAL EXPRE
4 OCTOBER 2003 £1.80
BASS IN YER FACE!
SUPERGROUP
PORTRAIT COLLECTION
KINGS OF LEON ANNOUNCE NME TOUR!
The Brit Pac
10 bands that w
change your li
The Distiller
First review of the
explosive albu
CRACK! ACID! ECSTASY! THE MARS VOLTA COME CLEAN
KERRANG!
www.kerrang.com
LIFE IS LOUD
SEPTEMBER 27 2003
£1.90
ROCK BOTTOM! WHOSE ARSE IS THIS?
Find out on page 50
You know you want it...
THE DARKNESS UNCOVERED
EAT LEAD, MOTHERF**KER!
SPINESHANK GO GUN CRAZY
TWINKLE TOES! DISCO DANCING WITH...RANCID?!
LOSTPROPHETS UK TOUR EXCLUSIVE!
PLUS
NINE INCH NAILS
PUNK ROCK POLITICIANS
JOSH HOMME
IRON MAIDEN
ARCH ENEMY
...AND A HOWLER MONKEY!
"DOES MY BUM LOOK BIG IN THIS?"
ROCK'S TOP 10 LADYBOYS EXPOSED
MUSE NEW ALBUM WORLD EXCLUSIV
KERRANG!
www.kerrang.com
LIFE IS LOUD
JUNE 21 2003/ £1.90
SKATING
BMX-ING
ROCKING
ROLL UP! ROLL UP! ROLL UP!
THE DARKNESS
& THE GREATEST SHOW ON EARTH!
ALSO STARRING:
METALLICA
GRILLED BY K! READERS! + LIVE IN PARIS
LINKIN PARK
COWBOYS, CARTOONS AND DANCE ROUTINES?!
ELECTRIC SIX
MURDER ON THE DANCE FLOOR...
EVANESCENCE
THEY'RE BIG, BUT ARE THEY FAMOUS?
SILVERCHAIR
HIP WIGGLING IN LONDON
PLUS
DONNA
POISO
THE WE
MAR
HOPPU
KITCHE
VIOLEN
DELIGH